THE WAY OF THE WORLD

The Way of the World
Benevolent and Malevolent Trends that Affect the Globe Today

By
Gregory James

E-BookTime, LLC
Montgomery, Alabama

The Way of the World
Benevolent and Malevolent Trends that Affect the Globe Today

Copyright © 2007 by Gregory James

All rights reserved. No part of this book may be reproduced or transmitted in any form or by any means, electronic or mechanical, including photocopying, recording, or by any information storage and retrieval system, without permission in writing from the copyright owner.

ISBN: 978-1-59824-448-9

First Edition
Published February 2007
E-BookTime, LLC
6598 Pumpkin Road
Montgomery, AL 36108
www.e-booktime.com

This book is dedicated:

To my father, who began as "just a farm kid from Nebraska" as he puts it. The journeys and successes of his life have shown me what is possible.

And to the great geographer, and my friend, Yi-Fu Tuan, in whose midst my ideas flourished.

Contents

Introduction 9
The Wave of Global Benevolence 13
Global Awareness 18
A Beacon of Light 25
Solar Energy 28
① Benevolent Organizations 38
Benevolent Individuals 47
② Organic Agriculture 57
③ Recycling 68
Negative Global Energies 77
Dependence on Oil 82
The So-Called "Drug War" 90
Human Traffic 97
④ The Gift of Tragedy 107

Bibliography 118

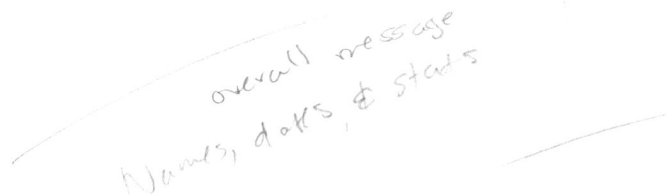

Introduction

There is so much going on in our world today: the globalization of culture and communication, an expanding environmental awareness, international peace treaties and altruism, and a move toward sustainable energy and agriculture – along with pollution and deforestation, wars over energy, an international sex trade, rampant starvation, widespread military aggression, and an exploding population... all of the good and the bad. And these realities are not random nor unexplainable. All trends observable on the globe today are sourced in either benevolence or malevolence. Said another way, everything that we see is sourced, at its root, in love or fear.

The energy of love expands, uplifts, heals, accepts, and includes, while fear restricts, diminishes, harms, attacks, and excludes. With these definitions it becomes clear which leaders, organizations, and decisions on the globe today are benevolent and based in love, and which are malevolent and based in fear.

Many in this world who have power and money are very fearful that they will lose it so they attack, subordinate, deceive, and hoard in order to maintain dominance. This is the principal source of fear and malevolence on the planet. Others who are in a position to help – and who have some awareness of the globe – have such a love for the world that they devote all of their ingenuity, skills, networks, and resources to the world's healing, recovery, and equitable pros-

Introduction

perity. This is the principal source of love and benevolence on the planet today. These two trends, feelings, or forces are the root of all that we see.

Outside of those who fear, deceive, and dominate, and those who help, uplift, and heal, are the majority of people in the First World who are fundamentally unaware. Most of us in the West (the First World) are living in relative luxury – plenty of food, leisure time, entertainment, and technological amenities. We have a vague awareness of the suffering, starvation, environmental crises, and war that most of the world is experiencing, but we feel no urgency to act and we may implicitly hope that these problems will simply work themselves out. We like to keep our attention on our lives and on this side of the world, yet these problems that we ignore are increasingly affecting the foundation of our own lives.

The inner workings of these levels of global society are a macrocosm of the inner workings inside each of us. We have the presentable, prosperous parts of us that we acknowledge and display – our new clothes, our smile, our job, our steady relationship – yet unacknowledged emotions and limiting painful beliefs are creating storms inside of us that go unseen and unchecked. These ignored parts of us are the cause of much suffering and of significant needs not being met. In both cases, the depleted and abandoned parts of us and of the world continue to shackle the progress of our larger Self.

We must first acknowledge these shadowed parts of ourselves and these shadowed parts of the globe for them to be brought to the light of day and healed. In order for this to happen we must shift our regular mode of operating. We must garner some sensitivity to ourselves and to the world. For a few millennia on the Earth, we have been living under the belief that advancement entails attack, aggression, and domination of one another. This is the traditional "male," or

Introduction

fear-based approach. Economic and military domination are how societies have expanded and furthered themselves. Yet this has left a few at the top and many more downtrodden and struggling to survive.

The new approach that is needed to remedy this has already begun to emerge. This traditionally "female" or love-based approach is grounded on the belief that compassion, cooperation, awareness, and inclusion are the foundation of all advancement and success. The rise of one uplifts another. The success of one group only adds to the success of others. This is the essential change: from basing our life choices on fear to basing them on love. This shift, as said, has already begun and it is the natural course of events: we as a planet returning to balance and returning to our nature as an interconnected, inter-loving whole. Yet still, this shift is in our hands and we must choose it in order for it to come to fruition. It is up to those who are aware and those who have the power to help. And so then, by that definition, it is up to you.

The Wave of Global Benevolence

The growing wave of positive energy which is uplifting and healing the world is comprised of the attitudes of love, compassion, and selflessness. This wave of benevolent energy is sourced principally in the first, or industrialized, world because a large portion of its population has achieved effortless subsistence and is able to shift its gaze to global-scale benevolent purposes.

The two main avenues of this love and compassion are short and long-term aid to the third world and the healing of the environment. Yet before these two avenues could become significant global forces, they were necessarily preceded by a raised global awareness. This expanded awareness, which is the foundation of the current tide of benevolence on the earth, is based on the evolution and improvement of technology. The internet, cell phones, 24-hour global news (CNN and BBC) have allowed us to be instantly connected to each other and to information all the time through virtually any medium. This instantly brought light to dark corners of the globe which made local injustices global issues. The globalization of culture – principally through American and Western music, television, movies, and fast food – with debatable pros and cons, has had the effect of creating a feeling of connectedness while fortifying English as the universal language. Finally, jet air travel, an albeit less recent technological innovation, has generated the world-changing possibility of traveling around the world in a matter of hours. The advent of this technology instantly removed any geographic barriers or limitations to the movement of people, products, and foods. This, again, had an immediate and astonishing effect on our awareness of each other.

This increased knowledge of the world spurred individuals, organizations, and governments mainly in the first world to offer help to the newly identified regions of need on the earth. Wealthy international philanthropists such as Ted Turner, Oprah Winfrey, Bill Gates, and Richard Branson have set a precedent for private benevolence with altruistic agendas that go beyond and offer a broader spectrum of help than traditional governmental aid. Nongovernmental organizations such as Greenpeace, the Sierra Club, Britain's OXFAM, Habitat for Humanity, the Red Cross, Save the Children, and literally thousands of others have taken it upon themselves to move the globe in a new direction and show compassion even in the face of much resistance. The United Nations is undeniably the most important benevolent organization on the planet whose effects toward nuclear disarmament, peace-keeping, and human rights assurance are changing the course of global societal evolution. Many nations in Europe offer support for the environment and are joined by the United States in their international protection of human rights.

The destinations of this philanthropy are short and long-term aid to the developing world, and the amelioration of the Earth's environment. Short-term aid is essentially food, housing, medical care and disaster relief for the most beleaguered regions and nations. This voluminous and ongoing relief attempts to help feed almost one billion undernourished people and provide shelter for the several hundred million with inadequate housing. The necessary complement to immediate relief is aid geared towards long-term recovery, redevelopment, and social equality. This includes programs such as sustainable organic farming education and start-up capital, establishing clean water supplies, financing infrastructure development such as highways and railroads, and setting up domestic human rights abuse monitoring organizations. Long-term assistance is provided by, notably, the Peace Corps, Human Rights Watch, and several groups contracted by the United Nations to provide localized assistance.

The natural systems of the earth, that is, the environment, is the other main recipient of this love and aid from benevolent individuals and organizations. Non-governmental organizations such as the Sierra Club, Greenpeace, Earth First!, and the World Wildlife Fund have been protecting the environment for several decades. They promote environmental causes on both the local and global scale – from protecting one tract of land from development to lobbying governments to sign international pollution reduction agreements. Their modus operandi, equally broad, includes grass roots volunteerism, regional environmental education promotion, and international advertising campaigns. Individual philanthropists have also had an impact on the environment. Ted Turner is a true environmentalist, donating hundreds of millions to environmental efforts in his lifetime. Richard Branson, owner of Virgin Airways, has pledged $3 billion of his company's profits to help fight global warming.

As a result of these efforts, organic agriculture has a significant presence in the U.S. and Europe as well as a growing presence in the developing world, solar power is the fastest-growing energy source on the planet, and recycling programs in the Western world – already informally practiced throughout the third world – have made recycling a way of life in countless cities and nations. Moreover, there has been a proliferation of international treaties which curb pollution, nuclear and industrial waste, and fossil fuel use.

Short-term and long-term aid to third world economies and people is having the combined effect of allowing inhabitants and nations to get back on their feet, as it were. With their immediate needs met, developing world denizens and organizations can invest themselves in collaborative projects with aid organizations such as sustainable agriculture, infrastructure building, and economic development and industrialization aimed at an earnest participation in the global economy. These ameliatory trends are fortifying these nations and helping to curb the massive flow of millions of people from the over-burdened countryside to cities in search of food and jobs. Industrialization also encourages a reduction in birth rates, while an assurance of basic human rights has positive effects on all levels of society. When these nations become self-sustaining, healthy, productive societies, then they can finally begin to give to the world their true gifts, their unique contribution to the global, cultural, and economic potpourri. With most of the population of the globe now living in the so-called "developing world," the latent potential for social, cultural, and natural expansion and development is awesome. Hence a more appropriate name for this burgeoning part of the globe is "the latent world." When these nations step into themselves and their role in this new age, then an egalitarian give-and-take and mutual uplifting will occur with the rest of the world. A focus on family sanctity, community-based identity and problem solving, and a harmony with nature, for instance, can be communicated from the latent world to the developed world where a return to this foundation is needed. In this way, the latent world can serve as the "roots" of global society, while the technology, democracy, and environmental awareness of the first world could be the "wings." Yet these traditional roles will dissolve as equal exchange and mutual acknowledgment increases. As the suffering and overlooked injustices of the developing world are brought to the light of day,

The Way of the World

and as these nations rise and express their true potential, they will display and fulfill their part of the evolving global cultural mosaic. The first world will begin to acknowledge the invaluable presence of the latent world and every part of the globe will see that they each fill an important role in the experience of our collective greatness. Likewise, as the globe becomes increasingly involved in the protection of its environment, governments and corporations will begin to broaden their goals beyond immediate profit to the greater good of humanity and long-term harmony with the environment.

From this new social and environmental perspective comes the realization that we are all a part of the same larger whole, an amalgam of diverse cultures in a living relationship and harmony with the Earth as our home. An acceptance and reverence for each other and for the Earth naturally ensues. And the final stage of this beautiful expansion of benevolence on the globe is a feeling of love and acceptance for every human, by every human, and a conscious collective decision to remain in a state of harmony and appreciation with the Earth.

Global Awareness

"Awareness is the best friend of the environment and the common good and it is the greatest enemy of avarice, abuse, and injustice."

—— Joy Palmer, February 2003

The most important benevolent trend on the earth today is an expanding global awareness. We are becoming more aware of each other and more aware of what is going on with nature, society, economics, war, and injustices across the globe. This is critical because evil and injustice cannot exist in the light of awareness. In darkness, iniquity, disease, and conflict fester and grow, much like bacteria grows in a dark, cold cellar or cancer flourishes in the body of an unexamined psyche and ignored soul. This light is the remedy to all darkness, and so it is critical to our healing and evolution as a planet. And all we must do is expose these evils and shift our gaze upon them and the healing and transformation shall rush in. All we must do, literally, is communicate with each other, interact with each other, and become aware of each other. In this way, the injustices in the world will be exposed and they will cease to have power and growth. A festering wound needs to be rinsed and cleansed. A plaguing memory needs to be reexamined, accepted, and released. Massive personal and national debts need to be acknowledged and dealt with. And social and environmental injustices need to be brought to the light of day. Our expanded

The Way of the World

awareness and connectedness is growing through several clear mechanisms: improved transportation, improved communication, an expansion of the omnipresence of news media, and a globalization of culture.

The principal method of transportation which connects us now more immediately and consistently is jet air travel. Now all regions of the globe are accessible within a few hours. Loved ones can be reached, wars can be photographically documented, environmental catastrophies can instantly be videod and analyzed. Jet air travel brings products, people, and foods immediately to their desired locations, so we experience a blending, a cross-pollination, a unification of the globe in a direct physical, visceral sense.

Improved communication, principally through a proliferation of cell phones and access to the Internet, has radically changed how and how *much* information flows. Three of the most common uses of the Internet are for e-mail, access to news, and investigating and booking travel arrangements. All three of these activities directly foster an awareness of our fellow man. In Western and industrialized countries, these technologies are more prevalent, yet they have a presence in essentially every global region. In 2002, there were 298 million cell phone users in the European Union, which is 79% of the population. In some locations, such as Luxembourg, there are more cell phones than people (1). In the same year, there were 135 million people in Europe who used the Internet, which is one-third of the total populace. Moreover, 90% of schools in the region have an Internet connection. Worldwide there are 112 million generic Internet hosts, which are computers that are permanently connected to the web.

The Internet fosters new non-territorial communities, which shatter spatial considerations and conceptualizations of a community or nation. It allows for the safe, constant, and mass-scale human interaction that form part of the foundation of a global connectivity and awareness. Yet taken to an extreme, this feeling of belonging to a cyber community can be disorienting.

"In an age where people have more opportunity to be interconnected across space and time through technologically-aided communication than during any other period in history, the (post) modern individual in contemporary Western society is paradoxically feeling increasingly isolated. New ways to understand and experience meaningful togetherness are being sought" (2).

This feeling of isolation brought on by techno-proliferation, however, can be cited as the source of another positive trend on the globe, which is a reconnection with the local. This "tribalism" if you will, and deliberate return to local social, economic, and cultural entities is paralleled by the huge recent rise in localized energy and food production. Solar energy is the fastest growing energy source on earth, due in large part to the fact that it can be received on an individual or community scale without dependence on a centralized fossil-fuel burning energy plant or the costly infrastructure which that entails. Organic farming in line with nature for local consumption is also growing very rapidly in the United States and Europe, and in much of the population-dense third world due to the environmentally harmful wake of large centralized chemical intensive agri-business.

Another facet of our ever-expanding awareness and unification as a globe is the globalization of culture, which has become synonymous with the Americanization of culture. The United States dominates all media. American movies are seen in almost every country on earth, and they often take in more money and usurp more screens in foreign countries than movies produced in that home country. Even in epicurean cultural fountains like France, American blockbusters are shown in the majority of theatres. American TV

The Way of the World

is no different. 75% of all purchased non-domestic TV programming in the world is from the U.S. That is, if a country buys TV from another country, three-fourths of the time it is from the U.S. (3). Moreover, 18 of the all-time 25 best-selling musical artists are American, including Garth Brooks with 104 million album sales, Elvis Presley with 86.5 million, Madonna with 59 million, and Michael Jackson with 58 million (4). Another cultural phenomenon, MTV, has, in the words of *Jihad vs. McWorld* author Benjamin Barber, become the true Trojan horse of American culture in foreign societies. Ten years after its inception in the late 1980s, MTV was being broadcast to 201 million households in 77 countries. By 1995 the vast majority of nations in the world, barring a scattering of inland developing world nations, had MTV or a similar domestic reproduction of it (5).

Another technology, the satellite dish, is an important factor in this trend. American TV can now find its way into foreign cultures – even isolated, traditional, or authoritarian ones. The radio waves go over walls and through centuries-old traditions, right into the living rooms of citizens. Like solar energy collectors, satellite dishes do not require expensive ground line infrastructure. They are independent, powerful, and localized. Star TV, a satellite network owned by Rupert Murdoch who also owns all FOX networks, is shown to 300 million viewers in Asia, while the Eutelsat satellite system sends programming to Europe, the Middle East, and North Africa and into 52.6 million homes (6). Moreover, author Lane Crothers states that:

"As satellite systems proliferate, they need to fill the immense bandwidth on which they broadcast. Ready-made and already proven popular (on movie screens), American programming provides easy filler. Under such circumstances it is reasonable to expect American television programming to proliferate globally in coming years" (7).

That the substance of American society has come to infiltrate and dominate the globe is well established. Traditional cultures are bending and yielding to its momentum, power, and likeability. Yet conversely, the source of this culture – America itself – is a cultural amalgam from around the world. We are a microcosm of the world. Except for the Native Americans, everyone in the U.S. is a fairly recent immigrant, the vast majority of us being here for less than six generations. Hence, we are all "from another country." And so American culture is necessarily a fresh and multi-influenced, dynamic cultural package that is being broadcast out into the world. In this way, we are globally united under a unilateral cultural essence which is being beamed out into the world, and that essence is a mix, blend, and almost democratic representation of the societies which are receiving it.

The last development or entity which is the fuel for our augmenting knowledge of the world and of our neighbors is the omnipresence of the media. Ted Turner's gutsy venture to provide the first 24-hour news channel on TNN proved a huge success and changed the role and scope of news media forever. It changed how governments and citizenry interact. It empowered citizens by giving them a voice and a window to the world, while simultaneously making governments accountable for their actions and policies. The recent expansion of news media presence and programming, perhaps more than any other modern entity, has shed this light of awareness across the earth. The prevalence and nature of genocide, military action, and human rights abuses in particular, were immediately affected. This new-found power of the media to effect real change and influence popular knowledge and opinion to such a degree has also come with responsibility. News networks are in a privileged position to help guide public awareness and shape our knowledge of the world. Their shaping of statistics, images, and the perception of events has enormous power to reconcile, heal, and ameliorate political, environmental, and social injustices. A shift from sensationalism – the pursuit of blood, conflict, and shocking footage at any cost – and toward a responsible investigation and delivery of the core of events with an intent to actually help and not just observe is crucial.

There is already evidence of this transformation in both news and other media forms as these groups are accepting their new role with a willing, albeit often profit-driven, air of social responsibility. CBS producer Mark Johnson pulled a violent criminal series called "Falcone" in the months following the Columbine school bloodshed. MTV banned guns in videos some years ago, and in 1998 began a movement against violence recognizable by the slogan "Take a Stand Against Violence." And resultingly, violence actually shows signs of losing its public cachet. "The public, through ticket sales, showed it is no longer interested in that," remarked president of Lion Gate Films, Peter Strauss. Television shows that have been described as dealing positively with trauma, violence, and displaying realistic pathways to healing are: Boston Public, 7th Heaven, Once and Again, Beverly Hills 90210, Buffy the Vampire Slayer, and Freaks and Geeks (8).

The ability of increased communication, transportation, globalization of culture, and media exposure of world events to spread awareness – and hence light – into every corner of the globe is immense indeed. Amidst this expanding interconnectivity, there is already evidence of a collaborative responsibility among those who have the power to effect change. The television and movie industries, along with news networks, are finding that highlighting the positive and noble aspects of people and events is beneficial both for political and social coherence as well as for ratings and sales. This so called "Oprah Winfrey Factor" of focusing on and cultivating the good in people and institutions is simple, yet nothing less than a grand-scale transformation of our planetary focus. Becoming aware of iniquity and "what's wrong'" with our planet and letting it heal, together with a nascent focus on what is right and inspiring and beautiful in the world constitutes perhaps the most beneficial reconciliation of our conscious power to better the world in our collective history.

When the light of awareness and attention on the positive coincides with the darkness of mistreatment and injustice, there is no contest. The battle is already won. Because, as paraphrased from a comment made by Albert Einstein in response to a professor's question in college, "There is no true darkness, only the temporary and perceived absence of light."

A Beacon of Light

The culture and ethos of the United States is unique on this planet. Our spirit of ambition, innovation, and our ability to think big is continually changing our reality and expanding our notion of what is possible. In a world full of rich traditions and cultures that have developed over centuries, what is proffered by the U.S., a mere babe of 200 – some years, is a fresh, uplifting experiment in casting history away and creating the future with inspired abandon. American culture vibrates with excitement and greatness and bursts with abundance, self-expression and vibrance. These feelings are an example of the desire of all human beings to be bigger, to be *more*, and so our nation elicits the most intrigue and attraction on the globe. Our products are tangible representations of this energy, this lifestyle, and the world cannot get enough of them. Our Nikes and Levis and MTV let people purchase or consume a piece of America, a tiny part of our world. Our movies and television programs and music broadcast our way of life to the world. Our icons become the world's icons, and what they wear and drink and say instantly become desired commodities. Everyone likes to dream. Our movies help us to vividly dream. They transport us from our daily mundane struggles and show us a better life, and an exciting or poignant existence.

    The world wants to feel exceptional, special, grand. But perhaps even more, people all over the world want to feel *cool*. And there is no cooler place than "the States." The

U.S. shows us that when we risk greatly and trust in ourselves, anything is possible. This is not to say that this nation is devoid of problems. We are not perfect – certainly imperialistic, perhaps avaricious, a bit oblivious to the rest of the world, and to varying degrees – wasteful. Yet what is GOOD about this country is indispensable and invaluable. This nation is the football star who's also an A student. He likes to party a bit too much but he's got a nice car and everybody wants to be like him. Most attractive of all – he's got a bright future. And that's all anyone or any country wants to know – that the future looks bright and much good is on the way. For this reason, the United States is a truly great country.

And sometimes, when you are uninspired or downtrodden or taught that you are less, or you've been suppressed by thought and physical control and limitation for so long – sometimes it is challenging to see the greatness in yourself. So it can be helpful to first see the greatness in another. This uplifts you and lets you know that greatness does indeed exist, which is a major leap of perspective to one who is truly downtrodden. And when they see this greatness, they know that it is possible. And by experiencing our movies and products and national passion, they see our success and they can begin to envision their own success. This boost, even though from without, engages something deep within. The parts of people that are naturally vibrating at this level move, stir, and come alive. When these feelings of magnificence within them are expressed, they are a unique and beautiful gift to the earth. These gifts are something that cannot be found anywhere else on the planet. When all worlds, all nations, all cultures, all individuals start to engage their own magnificence, the bounty and abundance and diverse richness of amazing, extraordinary creations will pour forth. We will be reminded of how much latent potential that this globe possesses.

The Way of the World

Italian cars, French food, Swiss banks and watches, Thai hospitality, Japanese precision, Brazilian sensuality, African community, Chinese stability, American ingenuity – these are all unique offerings. And when you produce what you are best at, you do it abundantly and with joy, and you will receive abundance in return. Eventually when all individuals and nations freely, joyfully give their gift to the world we will no longer need artificial exchanges mediated by money, because all gifts and talents will be given freely. We will be blessed and supported by the unique, joyful creations and services of others, and they will be supported by ours. A farmer cannot eat all of his apples, so he offers them to the community. A teacher requires students in order to share her gifts, and a doctor has no purpose without people in need of healing. Giving and receiving are a part of the same whole and because of this, all needs are naturally met. This is our destiny as a planet and it is not too far away.

Solar Energy

Throughout history the world has satisfied its energy needs through a wide array of sources: wind power for ocean voyages, animal power for agriculture and transportation, the heat of the sun to warm us and allow plants to grow. In the past two centuries, the globe has developed an addiction to a new form of energy – the burning of fossil fuels in the form of coal and petroleum. Today we are experiencing massive environmental degradation due to pollution and global warming, large-scale wars waged over energy (oil), and a monopolization of global wealth and energy by only a few Western oil companies. All of these observable trends are directly linked to one phenomenon: dependence on fossil fuels. Fossil fuels have served our needs for some time, but for hundreds and even thousands of years, a better, cleaner, and limitless form of energy has been ever present – the energy of the sun.

In the words of author Frank Kryza, "Harnessing the sun's energy is one of human kind's oldest fantasies, ranking with perpetual motion and the transmutation of base metals into gold" (1). The ancient Greek academician and engineer Archimedes set fire to enemy ships with the reflected light of the sun. Leonardo da Vinci proposed the idea of solar power being used for commercial purposes. 19th century inventor Frank Shuman built a massive solar powered plant which pumped 6,000 gallons of river water per minute onto cotton fields above the Nile. After Shuman's great success in Egypt, many thought solar energy was poised to make a big transition into popular usage. (2)

In February of 1914 just before the outset of World War I, Shuman wrote in *Scientific American*: "Sun power is now a fact and no longer in the "beautiful possibility" stage... (It will have) a history something like aerial navigation. The Wrights made an "actual record" flight and thereafter developments were more rapid. We have made an "actual record" in sun power and we also hope now for quick developments" (3).

Shuman's invention and his optimism were as impressive and real as the potential for solar power to be adopted across the world at that time. But those plans were washed away by the coming of World War I. Immediately a high-powered, dense and mobile form of energy was necessary, so oil took precedence over solar, and notably, over coal power as well. The urgency and ravages of war quickly overshadowed the beauty and simplicity of solar power. The current political climate on the earth is again tumultuous enough to pull our attention from the simple, clean, bountiful gift of solar energy, but the environmental decline that we are witnessing is necessarily waking us up to the need for sources of clean and renewable energy.

The utilization of solar energy is practical, economical and inevitable. Its benefits are impressive. Solar energy is limitless, because in a few days the sun showers the earth with enough energy to supply our energy needs for an entire year. It is totally environmentally friendly, and virtually free after the construction and installation of solar-receiving apparatus. It allows all countries to have their own sustainable, independent energy source, which promotes self-sufficiency and helps to balance the global wealth gradient. And unlike fossil fuels, solar power requires very little transportation and distribution. Because solar energy can be stored in batteries or in the existing electric power grid, the variability of sunny or cloudy days becomes a non-issue. It does not pollute the environment, which curbs the effects of global warming and allows the atmosphere to "heal." Also, wars for oil and energy will no longer be necessary because solar energy is available in every global region. The benefits of solar energy are so grand that they are difficult to absorb: Limitless energy forever, zero pollution forever, ubiquitously available, and after some basic construction, virtually free forever. No more wars over energy, no more digging or searching for oil, no more pollution from energy production, and very soon, no more high prices to heat our homes or fuel our cars.

Much scientific and social debate transpires about the practicality and utility of solar versus fossil fuel power. Yet in reality, both solar energy and fossil fuels are simply sunlight stored in different forms. Fossil fuels are the degraded, condensed decay of millions of years of fossils – that is – plants and animals. Plants survive by converting the sun's energy into chemical energy through photosynthesis, and animals survive by consuming this stored energy in plants. Therefore, the "life force" in plant and animal remains, or fossils, is simply ancient, degraded, condensed sunlight. This is petroleum, or oil. "Solar energy" as such is simply captured and utilizable sunlight in its highest and purest energy form. If you will, solar energy is "fresh" and undegraded energy from the sun. The fact that using fresh solar energy generates essentially no negative effects on the environment, while burning decayed, old solar energy pollutes the air, damages living things, and is causing the globe to heat up are clear signs from nature guiding us to the best, fresh form of the sun's power. Another critical point is that solar energy is limitless, while fossil fuels will soon run out.

The European Union estimates that two billion people worldwide are not connected to the electric power grid. They are ideal candidates for the localized, cheap solar energy collection process, since extending the traditional power grid infrastructure is prohibitively costly. Accordingly, countless solar energy projects are springing up in the developing world, principally for water pumping and electric lighting. Solar energy production is growing worldwide by 29% per year, and it is being adopted in locations which generally have three characteristics: 1) ample sunlight, 2) existing expensive grid-based electricity, and 3) government incentives for solar energy facility construction. In Japan, Germany, and the American Southwest, photovoltaic (PV) electricity is already utilized by hundreds of thousands of denizens, while 150 schools in Germany now use Photovoltaic systems for their energy needs (4). The US Coast Guard has 10,525 "stand-alone" PV systems, each saving taxpayers an estimated $5,000 over its lifetime, while Zaire's 20-building Bulape Hospital is the world's first medical complex that is 100% solar powered (5). Near Barstow, California, there is a 300-foot tower encircled by almost 2000 giant mirrors, called heliostats, which reflect the sun's heat to the center of the tower. This generates ten megawatts of power, which is enough to light 6,000 homes in Southern California. Moreover, by 1991, PV systems were used by 35 U.S. utility companies (6).

Renewable energy in general, including hydroelectric, wind, ocean, and solar power, is growing very rapidly. Iceland's use of geothermal and hydroelectric energy is advancing to the point that they are flirting with being the globe's first society/economy that is free of fossil fuels entirely. In 1993, renewable energy already produced 10% of the total US energy supply. 6% of all new electricity-generating facilities in 2004 were for wind power, and wind power is growing at 20% annually across the globe. The UK, Denmark, and Germany lead the world in this category (7). By the year 2030, some estimates suggest that renewables could supply up to 70 percent of America's energy needs (8). Biomass energy generation, or burning plants and wood, is also a significant source of energy, and accounts for up to half of renewable energy production in some regions. All renewables are excellent alternatives to fossil fuels, yet solar energy clearly has the best potential to replace fossil fuels in the foreseeable future. This is true for three reasons: solar energy has zero emissions, no moving parts, and it is available essentially everywhere. This translates to virtually no maintenance and no need for energy distribution after collection.

There are several practical aspects to the adoption of solar energy. PV technology can be paid for by including it in the mortgage of homes and commercial buildings, making its cost virtually disappear, since it will account for only one to ten percent of the purchase price. Renewable energy production facilities are much faster and cheaper to construct than traditional energy production facilities. Renewable energy stations are constructed in half of the time, for instance, of nuclear facilities. Photovoltaic systems take a maximum of a year to install on a commercial or industrial scale. Nuclear facilities normally take between seven and twelve years to be completely constructed and functional. Residential and commercial solar users can be connected to the traditional electric grid so that nighttime use of electricity can be provided by traditional fossil fuel burning plants, and will not require expensive battery units to be purchased by homeowners. This is critical, since the electric grid was called the greatest invention of the twentieth century by the National Academy of Engineering in 2000, and being able to synergize with this technology makes solar an easy fit with existing energy infrastructure. In addition, solar panels, like electric cars, are very low-maintenance because they have only one moving part. This also makes them very reliable. Last, photovoltaic energy collection works reliably in essentially all climates and all latitudes. That is, as already stated, it is ubiquitously available.

Some social benefits of solar energy are that each household, region, and nation has good energy security and therefore is not dependent on other people or nations for energy, which can decrease war. Also, solar power collection in rural areas can help to stem the current deluge of rural-to-urban migration in the developing world by bringing a coveted urban amenity – electricity – to isolated households (9). Most beleaguered nations in the sun-drenched tropics will have the greatest potential for energy production from solar, and they don't need expensive infrastructure to distribute it, which is not true with oil or grid-based electricity. Having locally produced clean, cheap electricity would greatly accelerate the demand and practicality of electric cars and hydrogen cars, because essentially there would no longer be a need for gasoline.

The globe uses energy much faster than we replenish it. In 1990, the total amount of energy consumed worldwide was equivalent to 7.5 billion metric tons of oil (10). 40% of this energy comes from oil, 23% from natural gas, 22% from coal, and about 8% from the renewable resources of water, wind, and sunlight (11). The United States has only 5% of the world's population yet consumes 25% of its energy, making us the biggest energy consumers and wasters on the planet. The globe burns oil, coal, and natural gas at alarming rates, all of which are non-renewable resources. Thus the concept of renewable energy – essentially energy from the sun and from the movement of wind and water – is so attractive.

In his book, *Solar Revolution*, Travis Bradford cites two economic forces that are generating change in the energy industry. One – modern industrialized and developing economies are experiencing increasing costs and risks of acquiring traditional energy supplies in the form of environmental degradation and military action to secure oil. Two – industrial economies will move away from centralized energy production to more localized and smaller production sites, which lends itself well to solar and other renewable energies (12).

An interesting perspective on the energy equation is that in conventional power plants, we burn a degraded form of solar energy (oil) to generate heat, which drives engines, which stimulate mechanisms which then produce electricity. Yet we could just leave out these intermediary steps and convert fresh, clean solar energy directly into electricity through the photovoltaic process.

The negative aspects of conventional energy production, that is, the burning of fossil fuels, are myriad. Severely deleterious political implications arise by relying on foreign energy and needing to incite military action in order to acquire that energy. Besides attracting harmful public opinion from the oil-producing regions, which could be said to fuel (in part) terrorist attention, these wars also destabilize nations in an already unstable region. Also, massive amounts of tax dollars are spent on these unnecessary wars, and on acquiring and distributing new oil. Hundreds of billions of dollars have been spent on the Iraq war alone, which any analyst would agree is related to the acquisition of oil. Hence, the taxpayers ultimately foot the bill for these ventures. Moreover, the burning of oil and coal produces massive amounts of carbon dioxide which is polluting our bodies, our air, and our environment. This pollution is producing the greenhouse effect which is a direct cause of global warming.

In "The Greenhouse Effect" published by Greenpeace, they state that if we continue with current levels of resource use and environmental degradation, "the world will be unlike anything in human history." They mention that massive climatic change along with changes in ocean temperatures and currents would cause rampant species extinctions worldwide. In the U.S. specifically, large areas of eastern and southern forests may be destroyed, and the Midwestern grain belt would become a desert (13).

These deleterious effects which come hand-in-hand with fossil fuel usage must be calculated into the overall equation of energy use, practicality, and cost. Authors Martin Katzman and Travis Bradford describe these "extra" aspects as "social costs" and "loaded costs," respectively (14). They include that these costs must be taken into account by those who decide on energy policy, and by the general public who ultimately decide which energy source to use. Many oil advocates emphasize that the initial cost of conversion to solar energy will be impractical and expensive. Yet these advocates should realize that the globe is already converting, but in another way – we are converting to a globe with rampant pollution, rising sea levels, perennial wars over energy, and skyrocketing asthma cases from pollution and skin cancer levels from ozone depletion. Author Jennifer Carless adds that since national security is such an issue of late, then energy self-sufficiency should be our first goal, because then the need for foreign military invasion would profoundly diminish (15).

When this broader view of the energy equation is taken into account, then it is projected by many that the conversion to solar energy will be precipitously fast. "Increasingly and dramatically over the next few decades... consumers will turn directly to the sun for their energy. This will happen not because solar power is clean and green but because basic economic and political reasons compel us to make this choice. At the point that the out-of-pocket real cash cost of solar electricity drops below the costs of current conventional energy alternatives (a situation that is already occurring in the Japanese residential electricity market), the adoption speed of solar energy will rival nearly every technological leap in history" (16). Being a major source of resistance to the solar age, oil company fears could be assuaged by the prospect of shifting their ingenuity and capitalist desires to the development of the most efficient and marketable photovoltaic cells. Defense contractors as well, in lieu of building war machines (which will largely be unnecessary when we stop fighting wars for oil) could build wind farms or harness geothermal energy (17).

War, global instability, and avarice of those who control energy and resources have delayed the world's conversion to solar energy for many decades. Frank Shuman's progress with solar power in the early 1900s was stymied by the chaos and instability of the first World War. Today is little different. We are perennially posited in a state of war and fear of war. This generates feelings of protection, territorialism, and divisiveness: an environment which favors the providers of existing and familiar channels of energy. In 19th century Europe, despite supply limitations, plant strikes, and other problems with coal, European rulers and governments did not seek out alternative sources of energy but instead "hunkered down" and did their best to control and monopolize all that was left of this dwindling resource (18). This is precisely what is happening with oil today. Environmental damage, wars, and escalating oil prices are demonstrating that the end of the oil age is arriving. Rather than acknowledging the ubiquity, environmental affinity, and low cost of solar energy, the oil giants are helping to promote gas-guzzling vehicles, actively suppressing any link between fossil fuels and global warming, and squeezing every last penny out of their brief and lucrative monopoly. It is difficult to peer through the fog created by so much distraction, conflict, and escalated demand surrounding oil, but it is the prerogative of individuals and leaders, especially in the powerful and resource-consumptive West, to see through this haze. The time has come to consciously and definitively

The Way of the World

take global energy in a new, benevolent, sustainable direction. That clear direction is solar power.

Benevolent Organizations

Improved technology, transportation and communication have lead to much more international awareness on the globe. Interdependent economies, governments, and cultures blended across borders have blurred the former traditional boundaries between nations, and an interconnected globe is emerging. One effect of this increased awareness and connectivity is that the "haves" are made aware of the "have nots," and this has spurred a wave of individual and organized benevolence across the globe. Amidst the emergence of this magnanimous spirit largely in the last fifty years, many national governments were still toiling in the mire of territorial conflict, avaricious economic competitiveness, and a propagation of the concept of the "zero-sum game" in international relations. Therefore, many groups were born which went under, around, and beyond national governments in their efforts and implementations of helping to ameliorate some of the lack and injustice that was being witnessed in the world.

These groups can broadly be defined as benevolent organizations, but are most commonly referred to as "non-governmental organizations," or NGOs, due to their supernational nature. They are non-profit and generally private. Some are international, while others are national or local in focus. The attention and active care that they offer usually centers around a few archetypal topics: human rights, animals and the environment, developing the third world, women's issues, conflict resolution, and the promotion of peace. They can range in size and scope from a local after-school program for at-risk kids to Amnesty International with one million members in 100 countries to the United Nations, which, with its considerable power and an almost 200-nation membership, is the largest international benevolent organization in the planet's history. According to the Union of International Associations, in 2004 there were nearly 6,600 non-governmental organizations in existence (1).

To achieve their philanthropic ends, benevolent international organizations (BIOs) employ government lobbying, litigation, extensive scientific research, grassroots networking, and local and international education. In order to function optimally and effectively, BIOs must operate in union and collaboration with governmental organizations, the scientific community, big business, and local individuals. This reality has given rise to the term "trans-national advocacy networks" to describe the compilation of actors on many levels that come together to actualize a philanthropic project. This phrase is taken from the landmark work *Activists Beyond Borders* by Margaret Keck and Kathryn Sikkink. A perfect example of this is found in the development of the proposed highway system in the Brazilian state of Rondonia. The team enlisted to bring this project to fruition includes U.S. human rights and environmental NGOs, Brazilian anthropologists, World Bank environmental staff and consultants, US congressional representatives, and media correspondents in the field of international environmentalism (2).

Most BIOs began as an outcry by an individual or small group of people against suffering or injustice that they were witnessing. The International Red Cross was begun by Henri Dunant, a Swiss merchant banker who followed Napoleon III onto the battlefield to get his approval for a business deal

(3). The unequaled carnage that he witnessed prompted him to organize local residents to pull bodies of the dead off the battle field and urged him to devote himself to stopping and assuaging the atrocities of war. OXFAM, a giant international aid organization, was initiated in WWII when British citizens established the Oxford Committee for Famine Relief. It came to be known by the organization's telegraph address – "oxfam." IVS, the International Voluntary Service, was a product of war-torn Europe in the wake of World War I. The Sierra Club's 700,000 members owe their allegiance to the club's founder, John Muir, a passionate and renowned conservationist and environmentalist in the early 20th century. This organization was once cited as "the most effective of the conservation groups" by political scientist Grant McConnell (4). Many philanthropic groups began in order to provide immediate assistance in times of war, famine, or conflict, but they soon saw that focusing their efforts at the cause of these societal ills would offer a much more lasting effect on these affected regions. This is when many organizations expanded from providing food, shelter, and medical attention to broader issues of human rights, environmental protection, and peace-building.

Even benevolent organizations whose scope does not extend beyond national boundaries deal with issues that are international: the environment, crisis aid, human rights, etc. and very few – if any – push nationalistic agendas. Therefore, an apt description of them could be Benevolent International Organizations, or BIOs. The precedent for BIOs was set centuries ago by the Catholic church in Europe and Buddhism in Asia. These institutions had considerable power and wealth and used much of it to ease suffering and hardship among their followers (5). The concept of tithing laid an important foundation for all charitable donations today which are the fuel for countless humanitarian efforts. Many landmark events and important movements in recent history were sourced in BIO (NGO) activity and ideology: the 1833-65 anti-slavery movement in the United States, the Geneva Conventions of 1864, the international women's suffrage movement from 1888-1926, the International Slavery Convention of 1926, and the 1920-23 campaign by missionaries and colonialists to end female circumcision in Kenya (6).

International aid in the form of money and resources has traditionally been left up to national governments and their en masse efforts to balance out the global wealth gradient. However, the arrival and maturation of sizeable BIOs in recent decades now provides a very necessary intermediary between these lump-sum flows of cash and their recipients. Larger BIOs such as the International Red Cross and Amnesty International have the staff and global ubiquity to absorb and effectively utilize large sums of money from government sources. Smaller BIOs, in turn, are often funded by these mega-organizations to implement more localized, personal scale distribution of these funds. Their presence on the ground and familiarity and grassroots connection to regions and local communities posits them as ideal husbanders of these beneficial funds and resources.

One way that resources are delivered to potential recipients is through "microcredit" low-interest loans to farmers and business people in the developing world. The average loan size in 2000 in Honduras, for example, was only $129 U.S. This prevalent mechanism for spurring economic growth is said to reach more than 25% of the applicable market in thirteen Latin American countries (7). The 2006 Nobel Peace Prize was given to Bangladeshi economist Muhammad Yunus for his landmark work with microcredit loans that centered on women as recipients. Benevolent organizations also receive funding from charitable foundations and from contracts for specific tasks from governmental programs or bodies such as the UN. BIOs on all levels, however, receive the majority of their funding from private individuals who simply write a check for their favorite cause. This is the most direct pathway for funds to flow from wealthy nations and individuals to poorer ones (8). In 2003 individuals in the United States donated $183.7 billion to charitable organizations (9).

Local and enthusiastic participation from local indigenous populations, relief workers observe, is critical to the success of any aid program. Cultivating support from individual donors at home and generating participation from locals at the relief site are both essential to the overall relief plight. One group that has immense untapped power and potential is the female population of these regions (10).

The latent labor and intellectual power of women is an unequaled resource in the developing world. Mahatma Ghandi once said:

"If only the women of the world came together, they could display such heroic nonviolence as to kick away the atom bomb like a mere ball. If the women of Asia wake up they will dazzle the world. My experiment in nonviolence would be instantly successful if I could secure women's help" (11).

On a macro scale, the interaction between benevolent international organizations and the United Nations has been beneficial for both players. The UN began as a peace-keeping body designed to intervene in conflicts and advocate peace, but they had little power to execute, implement, and maintain their decisions and accords. This power to implement and maintain came with the UN peace-keeping troops and with NGO (BIO) ground involvement. Cultivating peace and protecting human rights were soon found to be inseparable. In 1956, UN Secretary General Dag Hammarskjold spoke to a group in New York city about this link. Even though there were no human rights treaties in existence at that time, he pushed for human rights promotion and international legislation. He urged NGOs to join him in this plight and to investigate and record human rights violations the world over (12).

In Hammarskjold's honor, the UN created the position of High Commisioner for Human Rights in 1993. Today NGOs are an invaluable part of the UN body of international action. The total number of NGOs registered with the UN rose from 40 in the 1940s to 2614 in 2005. (13). The UN is the largest and most powerful benevolent international organization in history, so its direction and leadership are of the utmost importance. The United States has considerable influence with the UN – some countries would argue that the U.S. has *too* much influence. Therefore, it is critical that the United States recognize its power and influence over this world-leading benevolent body and acquiesce to some degree to its universal philanthropic agenda. This will require that the U.S. drop some of its self-focused economic endeavors in favor of utilitarian ones, but in doing this we will soon see that lifting up other nations can only lift us. A rising tide lifts all boats.

Some evidence of U.S. philanthropy was seen when U.S. assistant secretary of state for democracy, human rights, and labor, Lorne W. Craner recently outlined U.S. efforts to spread democracy and ameliorate human life in the Middle East, central Asia, and China. We as a nation have also recently created the "Five billion dollar millenium challenge account" which offers money to nations who show attempts to reform their economic, social, and political operations (14).

Some statistics that describe our modern globe make it obvious that large, effective, and powerful BIOs are needed. 800 million people suffer from malnutrition on the globe. 900 million are illiterate. Over one billion live on less than one dollar a day. Perhaps one-fourth of humanity lives in poverty. Organizations that are combating these bleak statistics are groups such as: Human Rights Watch, CARE international, OXFAM international, and the French Federation Internationale des Droits de l'Homme (FIDH). In the environmental realm, while 1.7 million species are known to exist, we lose approximately 50,000 a year due to deforestation and global warming. However, it is estimated that there may be as many as three to 50 million total species in existence, which would mean that proportionally we would be losing from 100,000 to 1.5 million species per year on the planet (15). Some agencies that are combating this loss are the Friends of the Earth International, Greenpeace, the World Wildlife Fund, and the Sierra Club.

Another group that has had a massive impact, mostly in the U.S. but also internationally, has been the Salvation Army. Begun as a religious crusade, the Salvation Army found that people cannot receive messages of spirituality if their basic needs are not met. The Salvation Army has since become one of the largest benevolent organizations in the US. Its senior program alone serves 25,000 clients annually. The Adult Rehabilitation Program serves 52,000 people annually and had accommodations for almost 12,000 in 1990 (16).

Some larger NGOs such as the World Bank and the World Trade Organization have policies which help the flow of capital and positively affect the developing world. Yet many of their 'missions' also have motives which are self-serving for powerful groups or governments in the first world. Overhauling or a supervised restructuring of these organizations may be beneficial. Worth mentioning, several businesses in the Western world have decidedly philanthropic ilks which are guided by the ethos of the company. Chick-fil-A, for instance, is owned by a Christian man, so the branches are closed on Sunday, and the company funds religious organizations and NGOs. Home Depot's founder believes in the entreprenurial spirit and funds fledgling businesses in the developing world (17).

The Way of the World

During the late 1990s, Amnesty International's secretary general had written indelibly on the whiteboard in her office: "advocacy, not impartiality" (18). This attitude is evidenced in the 2005 claim by the organization that Guantanamo (US Marine base in Cuba) was a "gulag," which prompted Secretary of Defense Donald Rumsfeld to respond and defend the White House publicly. The fact that it generated a public response from the U.S. government shows both that it struck a chord of truth, and that A.I. has enough credibility to be taken seriously on these issues. It also displays that NGOs are not necessarily pushovers and add some teeth to the larger benevolent movement. In this light, the international NGO body can be compared to the ancient mythical chimera – a beast fused from three other animals that made it a formidable foe. The body of the NGO chimera is the humanitarian aid and localized infrastructural development, the brains are its ability to research, educate, lobby government, and shape international policy, while the teeth of the NGO beast are displayed in the direct challenging of existing regimes through protest, sanctions, and media exposure.

The size, power, ubiquity, and effectiveness of Benevolent International Organizations is impressive and growing. Many magnanimous individuals and groups have brought these agencies and movements into existence and allowed them to evolve and prosper. They are particularly important and well-suited to this modern international scene because they are international, flexible, and broad-based. They are an immediate and tangible beacon of compassion for those who are desperate, those who are in need, and those who are powerless. Where governments or charitable foundations may delay in delivering rapid, visceral help, BIOs rush in to help with effective, established, and personal networks in needy regions and communities. NGOs give a man a fish *and* a fishing pole. On the other side of this battle, NGOs are at the helm in providing, to governments and the general public alike, the necessary research, education, and information about pervasive injustices and human suffering on the planet. This spread of information is perhaps the most critical element in alleviating the abuse of our environment and of our fellow man because awareness is the beginning of healing and it is the most powerful remedy for any evil.

In 1998, Pierre Sane gave a prophetic statement about Amnesty International which goes far to disclose the true nature of NGOs collectively and paints a positive future for the emerging benevolent nature of human interaction:

"Amnesty International was not established to free prisoners of conscience (prisoners of limiting ideas). Amnesty was established to contribute to the full realization of Human Rights for all." And the spirit behind the organization is "the benevolent influence of a universal, uniting, indomitable power usually referred to as compassion" (19).

Benevolent Individuals
The Oprah Winfrey Factor

Powerful, magnanimous, benevolent individuals are a critical part of the equation for the continuing and rapid evolution of this planet. Any individual has the power to uplift others. Some uplift their friend or spouse. Some uplift a classroom or a household. The will of a good quarterback can inspire a team to a victory, while the powerful spirit of a good preacher can lift a whole community. Individuals are needed and called upon at all levels of leadership and inspiration. Presidents and other national-scale leaders have innumerable times changed the course of their people's vision, focus, morale, or even their history. And there have been a few individuals who exhibited the power to uplift the entire world. We all know their names.

The power of individuals to uplift is mighty, and one way that they do this is through giving money – whether they are billionaires or bellboys. The Guggenheims, John D. Rockefeller III, and Andrew Carnegie financially supported everything from aviation and space rocketry to penicillin and guaranteed pensions for teachers. On the other side of the giving coin was the March of Dimes which was funded by the pocket change of literally millions of donors and resulted in the first polio vaccine (1). We in the United States are the most generous citizens in the world, in that we donate a much larger percentage of our GDP than the denizens of any other country. 89% of Americans made donations in 2001, totaling $177 billion (2).

Author Claire Gaudiani suggests that Americans are not generous because they are rich. Rather, that we are rich because we are generous (3). That is, philanthropy throughout the generations in this country has largely been directed beyond immediate aid and toward investing in our human and infrastructural capital. For instance, private donations sent many prominent Americans to college, such as Ralph Waldo Emerson, Alice Walker, Oprah Winfrey, Itzhak Perlman, and Bill Clinton. These people all went on to considerably enrich the lives of both Americans and citizens of the globe. Half of all hospital beds, 95% of all orchestras, and 60% of all social service organizations are funded by private individuals (4).

As a matter of course, many leaders and persons who uplift do so through action and not just through monetary donation. Often a tragedy or tragic era provides the opportunity for a true leader or hero to rise up. The Nazi reign in Europe and the era of slavery in the U.S. produced heroes such as Arthur Schindler and Elie Weisel, and Harriet Tubman and Frederick Douglass, respectively. In fact, noting the geographic source of historical "heroes" leads us to the most poignant sites of suffering. Mohandes Ghandi, Nelson Mandela, and Stephen Biko all originally fought for minority rights in South Africa, a hyper-segregated and highly discriminative country at the time. Martin Luther King, Malcolm X, and Marcus Garvey all fought for the civil rights of American Blacks in the separate but still unequal United States of the 1960s. Today we see prominent figures such as Oprah Winfrey, Al Gore, and Michael Moore who are changing the way we think and opposing the status quo. What does their prominence say about the current social climate in this country? What are they fighting against?

The Way of the World

Al Gore is primarily an environmentalist. As a citizen of one of the most environmentally irresponsible nations on earth, he is outraged at the way we and other industrialized nations are abusing the earth. Michael Moore is essentially a champion of government transparency. He is a powerful force toward galvanizing the public to take part in, or even just take notice of, the management of its country. That Moore's expose's are necessary and viewed on a mass scale is a testament to how shrouded and clandestine the operations of our government are. Oprah Winfrey's contributions to our society are many and far-reaching. If her main thrust had to be pinpointed, perhaps it is that she teaches us to look for and cultivate the good in people. In an era of barrages of negative news about wars and violence, and the propagation of fear of other countries, religions, and even our next door neighbors, Oprah goes against that tide and encourages us to expect and highlight the good in each other and in the world.

Specific events can also elicit and necessitate new ways of interacting with each other. The Hurricane Katrina and September 11 tragedies are such examples here in the U.S. These disasters were so large in scale that no individual, organization, or government could handle the care, reparations and recovery. We necessarily had to *collaborate* in order to significantly help. Organizations public and private, profit and non-profit, governmental and individual all came together to begin to repair our torn cities of New York and New Orleans. This showed us a precedent for how we must handle our nation and our world in the future...together. This topic is elucidated by "Collaborative Philanthropies" author Elwood Hopkins.

This confluence of different players to bring a larger goal into reality is becoming more common in corporate America. Target and the Salvation Army have teamed up to aid local communities, and they recently united with magician David Blaine in a large charity and publicity event. If

Blaine could find his way out of a spinning gyroscope by the morning of Black Friday – the day after Thanksgiving – Target would give several families a $500 shopping spree (5). (He did find his way out, incidentally). Another beautiful and encouraging example of philanthropic confluence is a trend whose pith is seen clearly in the television show "Extreme Makeover, Home Edition." Behind the façade of a home-makeover show, this giant production finds families with specific and deep needs and builds fully-amenitied homes for them in a single week.

This alone is an encouraging sight. But more encouraging is that all of the labor, appliances, and building materials are donated to the show and to each construction project. This, of course, is often in exchange for advertisement space on the show, which is naturally good for business. And that's the amazing part of it – there is now a precedent that being benevolent is good for business! That is a revolutionary, palpable, immediate, and emotional realization, as it is masterfully presented to us by the ABC/Extreme Makeover production team. Corporate philanthropy certainly has a tradition of benefiting a company's image, but never so profoundly, immediately, and effectively as through this particular medium and method. Examples like the Target/Salvation Army/Blaine and Extreme Makeover collaborations are blazing a trail for future altruistic efforts and setting an important precedent: that collaborative philanthropies can generate a cascade of varied and positive effects and, simply, that giving is very beneficial for everyone involved.

In many aspects of the recovery effort in these tragedies mentioned, individuals took the lead if and when the government showed a lethargic response. This is the exact reason for and vector of the power and necessity of the benevolent individual in our world today. Many governments are still engrossed in the lure of territorial and financial conquest through military action and economic subjugation. The United States has the positive effect of spreading ideas of equal rights and democracy, yet it has spent hundreds of billions of dollars on warring with a tiny Middle Eastern nation. So while many powerful governments are otherwise entoiled, powerful and magnanimous individuals have stepped up and taken it upon themselves to incite change.

Countless families and individuals throughout this country's and this globe's history have had a profound benevolent impact, from the Medecis of Renaissance Italy to the Guggenheims, McLeods, Fords, Rockefellers, Packards, Carnegies, and Kellogs of 20th century America. And in America today, a few salient individuals require a mention: Ted Turner, Bill Gates, Al Gore, Richard Branson, and Oprah Winfrey.

The philanthropy of Ted Turner in this century, in short, is amazing. He is a lively, outspoken, ambitious individual, a giant benevolent force on the planet, and often said to be almost childlike by those close to him. Turner amassed his fortune in the cable television and news industry. The innovator of 24-hour news, he saw his network's information delivery as a public service and he saw movies and cartoons (Turner classics on his TNT station) as able to carry TV viewers to "magical places" (6).

Christine Amanpour, who joined Turner's news station, CNN, in 1983, said "The idea of 24-hour news and global news is his creation. That's changed the world. It's changed people's relations with their governments. It's meant that governments can no longer crack down with impunity on protests" (7). Yet his service to society goes much further than magical movies and news channels. Turner has a deep desire both to protect the environment and to halt and reverse nuclear proliferation. His commitment to global peace is so great that in 1997, Ted Turner walked into United Nation's Secretary Kofi Anan's office and said "I'm going to give you a billion dollars." Which he proceeded to do, with a $100 million donation each year for ten years (8).

He is a tireless defender of and donator to environmental causes, giving hundreds of millions in his lifetime to such causes. In 2001 alone, the Turner Foundation gave almost $70 million to environmental causes (9). This portrait of magnanimity has also helped to spur other large-scale donations. Turner publicly urged other American billionaires to "loosen up their wads" which helped to jolt Bill Gates into a philanthropic state. Eventually Gates donated $25 billion, principally toward world health and the population explosion. Ted Turner is benevolent, powerful, outspoken, and caring, and he walks and talks with the same swagger as John Wayne in an old Western. He is a consummate philanthropist, and a likeable one at that.

Al Gore is known for being the former Vice President and was very nearly put into office as the President of the United States. Yet at his core, he is a defender of the environment. He cares for the soil, the water, the air, and the living inhabitants of the earth as if it were his personal responsibility to tend to them. His book "Earth in the Balance" was a wake-up call to many and a best seller, and it divulged his commitment to all things natural. Beyond just a wake-up call, Gore's documentary "An Inconvenient Truth" is a strong admonishment to those who play a part in the thrashing of our global environment and a universal call to duty for all to help heal it. Gore pushed for the "Triana" satellite to provide a constant live view of the earth, which had not been available since the 1972 Apollo mission, and would greatly facilitate in the identification and monitoring of global environmental problems (10). Al Gore has used his political celebrity completely unselfishly in order to bring awareness to the current beleaguered state of our environment and to spur the general public, corporations, and gov-

The Way of the World

ernments to take action to rectify that. Sir Richard Branson, British owner of Virgin Atlantic Airlines and Virgin Records, has also been a strong environmental advocate for years. He is investing $3 billion of his airline's profits to develop alternative clean-burning fuels and to fight global warming in general.

While there are many powerful and indispensable altruistic figures in the United States today, in this authors' opinion, this country's greatest philanthropist in the true sense of the word – a lover of man – is Oprah Winfrey. CNN and Time.com called her "arguably the world's most powerful woman." Business Week named her the greatest black philanthropist in U.S. history, and Time magazine cited her as one of only four people who have shaped both the 20th and 21st centuries. But what Oprah gives to the world goes beyond money or celebrity or any specific cause – she is simply a powerful loving presence, and an example of how to live. She has fully developed her personal capital, she is a spiritually-connected and self-expressed magnanimous individual, and moreover, she teaches us all to look for and celebrate the good in other people.

To date, Oprah's Angel Network has raised over $51 million. In 2005 she gave away $250 million of her own money, $10 million of that to the Katrina relief effort (11). She is building a girls' school in South Africa and she has spent $7 million putting 100 black men through college (12). The March 22, 2002 edition of Christianity Today called Ms. Winfrey "The Church of 'O,' a post-modern priestess – an icon of church free spirituality." Very simply, it just feels good to wake up and know that Oprah is in the world, and that she's up to something good.

The changes that these visionary leaders effect allow us to see that ideas and visions stimulate the confluence and coagulation of people and things to fulfill a larger goal and new realities. Paul Romer, a Stanford University economist, proposed the idea that an economy is founded on ideas rather than on tangible things (13). Those with good ideas are looking for the money to actualize their visions, while the wealthy are searching for deserving, ambitious individuals whom they can support. This union is what makes philanthropy so essential to the progress of a society. As mentioned before, Oprah Winfrey went to college on the donation of a private individual, and now her ideas and presence uplift millions or even billions. It is quite interesting and beneficial to a society when a member of the downtrodden rises to the level of "royalty." This is indeed part of the plan for the healing and re-balancing of the world today. The meek shall inherit the earth.

Witness the plight of black Americans. Their labor provided the foundation for the building of this nation's industrialization and 19th century economic dominion, yet they suffered harsh discrimination and second-class citizen status for centuries. Today, the black culture is so pervasive in America and the world, due largely to its dissemination through music, movies, and television, that it has become indistinguishable from American culture itself. That is to say that in many ways, black culture is now at the helm of American popular culture. Moreover, black women's financial, societal, and spiritual rise in recent decades has been remarkable relative to their contemporary cohorts. Their particular rise has pulled this country up by its bootstraps by lifting black women, who author Zora Neale Hurston called "the mule of the world," into a position of power, prominence, and leadership.

In 2006, the Mexican and Central American population in the U.S. is present on all socio-economic levels, though principally represented in the working class. They are now the backs that break each day to provide the labor and services that this country needs to thrive. Besides the wealth of Latino history and culture that has already benefited this na-

The Way of the World

tion, what significant contributions will this Latino community bring to this country in coming decades?

To conclude this idea of uplifting someone that they might uplift you in the future, a story about two young British boys may prove very encouraging. A wealthy family lived on a large 19th century English estate, and the estate grounds and home were tended to by a man and his wife and their children. The two families had sons of similar age and the boys would regularly play together. Despite not being able to swim, one day the wealthy boy jumped into the family pond, and immediately began to struggle to stay afloat. The other boy eventually saw this struggle and rushed in to save the young heir at the point of drowning. The parents were so thankful that they said to the servant father that they would fulfill any one request that he had, no matter how large. Having a strong belief in the importance of education, he immediately said "Send my son to medical school."

That young son of the estate-owning family eventually grew up to be Winston Churchill, and he led the entire nation to victory in World War II. One day during the early 1940s, in the thrust of the war, Winston drew quite ill. Quite fortuitously, penicillin had just been discovered by Alexander Fleming, a British doctor and medical researcher. Doctor Fleming himself was summoned to Mr. Churchill's side to administer the shot and assess his health. A few days later the doctor returned to find Winston up and about and healthy. At the wizened doctor's approach, Winston leaned close and whispered "That's the second time you've saved my life, Dr. Fleming."

We never know when our donation of love or money or support will be the footspring to another's greatness. Nor can we perhaps imagine what magnificence will be unleashed when we do so and how it will affect, or even save, our own life. On an individual, community, national, and global scale, this same dynamic is true. Benevolent individuals with great power to affect both persons and nations are a huge force in this necessary uplifting. And we all have this power, on some level. So as individuals and as a nation, who can we uplift now that will in turn raise us up in the future? Who among us is so gifted that they will change the way we live and think, if only we give them the start they need? What hero is waiting for your gift, your attention, your love? Are you the next great benefactor, or are you the hero who waits to bloom? Either way, now is the time to share your gifts with the world.

Organic Agriculture
Ensuring Future Harvests

Feeding the world is fundamentally and inextricably based on growing food, that is, agriculture. Both humans and animals are fed by food that grows out of the earth. Domesticated agriculture began about 10,000 years ago but has experienced massive changes in this most recent decade due to the astronomical rise in global population. Yields have had to increase, so mechanization and chemical aids became integral to many wealthy nations' food-cultivation practices. This approach, culminating in a sense with the Green Revolution of the 80's and 90s, proved very successful at increasing yields. Yet in its wake, with a few decades of perspective, the negative effects of this industrial scale agriculture are now observable – namely, pesticide and herbicide-contaminated soils, water supplies, and food, as well as topsoil loss on a grand scale, and a population that has consumed harmful chemical-laden food for years.

Due to these proven deleterious effects both on the environment and on the health of the general human population, a move toward agriculture that is in symbiosis with nature began. Organic agriculture – also called sustainable agriculture, low-input agriculture, biological agriculture, and traditional agriculture– is that symbiotic method. Employed most pervasively and extensively in Europe, organic agriculture is attractive essentially for its positive health benefits for people and for its beneficial effect and symbiotic relationship with the environment. It has become a $26 billion industry world-wide, and is growing at 15-30% annually (1).

Sustainable agriculture is also showing substantial growth in the developing world, with 90 developing countries now producing organic foods on a commercial scale. This trend is fueled by an increasing demand in the first world for organic tropical food products and by an immediate need to curtail the damage to soils and water supplies wrought by decades of intensive conventional farming in equatorial nations. Some support for this organic movement has come from national governments, but the lion's share has come from benevolent non-governmental organizations and regional affiliations which are committed to this movement. The lure of the simplicity and centralized profits of large-scale chemical or "conventional" farming in the United States is only gradually yielding to the attractiveness of the health benefits and environmental sustainability of the organic approach. Though it is growing significantly each year, organic production only accounts for 0.2% of total agricultural output in the U.S. (2).

Organic farming has a few essential characteristics. It is usually defined by what it does *not* entail. Very simply, organic farmers do not use chemical fertilizers, pesticides, herbicides, or genetically modified or engineered seeds. What organic farming *does* utilize in order to promote healthy, sizeable, and environmentally-feasible yields is three-fold: crop rotation and crop diversification, using only organic fertilizers in the form of livestock manure, "green manure" or crops tilled under the soil, and vertical integration – ownership, management, livestock, and labor all in one site (3). All of these methods support healthy, nutrient-rich soil as well as aiding in natural pest and weed control. Organic farms are also usually much smaller than conventional ones.

The Way of the World

Conventional farms are defined by huge acreages of mono-crops, heavy chemical additives such as synthetic fertilizers, pesticides and herbicides, and significant portions of yields coming from genetically modified or engineered seeds. Some positives of conventional or chemical farming are that it frees up a large portion of the population for other endeavors (which could be a positive or a negative), and it produces massive yields and surpluses which have helped in some part to feed starving populations. Yet its negative effects cannot be ignored. Economically, small and medium-sized farms are disappearing as are rural communities which exacerbates the already rapid rural-to-urban migration, especially in the developing world. Farms are over-subsidized by the government and so surpluses are produced and crop prices fall, thus necessitating larger yields and hence larger amounts of chemical additives to the soil the following year. Environmentally, synthetic fertilizers kill living biota, or humus, such as acidopholous and good bacteria in the soil, while pesticides and herbicides reside on food and filter into groundwater and streams, and eventually into the ocean. Massive amounts of unutilized manure (in giant non farm-related feed lots) also constitute a significant pollutant source.

Conventional farming, now termed "agri-business," has become inextricably and overwhelmingly motivated by money. Policy decisions seem to be made with complete disregard for the environment and only focused on larger and larger yields. In his book, *The Unsettling of America: Culture and Agriculture*, author Wendell Berry comments that "the economy of money has infiltrated and subverted the economies of nature, energy, and the human spirit" (4).

Another negative aspect of conventional farming is the proliferation of GMOs, or, genetically modified organisms. This refers to seeds that are genetically altered by splicing in DNA from other plants and even animals in order to give the seeds certain traits, such as resistance to certain pests or more resilience in drought. For instance, genes from a salmon may be inserted into a corn plant, or genes from a tuber may be spliced into a fruit tree. These seeds allow for higher yields and less need for adherence to nature's indices and cycles, yet it is unknown what effect these gene-spliced organisms are having on human beings. In organic agriculture, naturally, GMO crops are never cultivated. A large proportion of nations across the globe will not accept GMO crops because they are wary of the possible negative effects and leery of the lack of long-term testing on these relatively new plants. In the United States, however, GMO crops abound with 72% of all GMO crops on earth being grown in the United States. 40% of corn, 73% of cotton, and 81% of soybeans in the U.S. are GMO crops (5). GMOs are not labeled in the U.S. because the USDA curiously does not require the labeling of these foods, nor has the USDA done any long-term research on their effects on people or the environment.

Many of these biotech firms are substantial contributors to political campaigns, and the principal way that they make money is to "patent nature." That is, these companies must be allowed to artificially generate a biological product, patent it, and thereby have exclusive rights to sell it. No one can patent apple seeds or cow manure, so patentable laboratory-produced versions of them are generated, advertised as superior, patented, then sold. Biotech firms even spend millions on advertising which puts a positive "emotional" spin on genetically engineered foods (6).

Moreover, farmers are forced to sign contracts with major GMO corporations that state they will only use their brand of pesticides and that they will not use seeds bought one year on the next year's crop. Some farmers are even sued because they are caught growing GMO crops without a contract. This industry has now even produced "suicidal genes," which cause a seed to self-destruct after several

The Way of the World

months, ensuring that it can only be used for a given year's planting (7).

The Pesticide Action Network has stated, "While many potential human health and environmental impacts are associated with these crops, testing has been remarkably inadequate." (8). In the words of author Leslie Duram, "With no long-term safety studies, we've introduced these new genetically altered materials to our environment and into our bodies. We simply do not have the facts on GMOs, yet we are currently conducting a massive experiment on you, me, the rest of society, and our ecosystems. Organic agriculture and buying organic food are the only way to avoid being part of this global experiment...(which is) being driven by the profit motives of several agribusiness and pharmaceutical corporations" (9).

It is widely known that conventional farms receive billions of dollars in government subsidies (paid by taxpayers), and these subsidies are contingent upon the continuation of conventional farming techniques, often including the purchase of GMOs. Organic farming in the United States is not a recipient of such governmental aid.

Interestingly, in early 20th century Europe, organic agriculture struggled to survive against the powerful chemical companies. This conflict was expressed most vividly when the "bio-dynamic" agricultural movement was banned by the Nazis beginning in 1940 due to pressure exerted upon them by the German chemical companies (10). Like modern United States, the Nazi government was focused entirely on generating the largest agricultural output possible in order to sustain economic and political prosperity, with the environment being essentially ignored (11). Soon, observations of the deleterious effects of such agriculture were ubiquitous, which coupled with an expanded demand for healthier foods to spur a resurgence of sustainable, natural food cultivation in Europe. A similar conversion is happening now in the

United States, despite heavy and continued government support of chemical agribusiness techniques.

Due both to a resident environmental awareness and simply a desire for healthier food, the growth of sustainable agriculture and for its products is notable in Europe. In Switzerland, 11% of farms are organic. In Austria the number is 9% and in Denmark it is 6% (12). The demand for organic foods in Europe, especially in their cold winters, is so great that they have secured many developing world and otherwise warm climate sources for organic fruits and vegetables. This demand, in turn, has spurred organic production in developing countries because of its immediate profitability.

Besides just for immediate profit, many nations, especially those in the developing world with large populations, are turning to sustainable organic farming out of necessity. Immeasurable amounts of topsoil runoff alone, not to mention chemical residues on food and in the soil and water supply, is enough to scare many governments into trying more sustainable methods in hopes of feeding their large and rapidly growing populations. The high yields of conventional farming, especially under the Green Revolution, were a quick fix but now are proving quite unrealistic in the long run.

In China's Changjiang Valley, 2.4 billion tons of topsoil has been lost to surface runoff, prompting the United Nations Environment Program (13) to intervene and implement an eco-farming agenda. Shifting cultivation, terracing, and crop rotation and diversification are now utilized.

Over the past two decades, Cuba is a very encouraging example, to say the least, of an underdeveloped nation wholeheartedly and successfully adopting organic agriculture. They have enlisted their sizeable scientific community to conduct extensive research on organic farming methods since Soviet-subsidized conventional production proved environmentally unsound and unable to feed its population. Hundreds of regional facilities now produce bio-pesticides, which are natural bacterial and fungal diseases that kill insects. Cuba is the only country in the hemisphere, as of 1994, to use microbial antagonists on a large scale to counter soil-borne plant disease (14). Organic fertilizers, composting of garbage from cities, and humus production by earthworm composts are further evidence of Cuba's all-inclusive dedication to this agricultural modality. And their results have been convincing and very encouraging in displaying how rapidly and successfully a nation can transition from conventional to organic farming when the government and industry join forces in a unified decision to convert. In the case of Cuba, a communist country, government and industry are essentially one in the same. Cuban officials estimate that with this kind of unilateral decision, any nation can convert to 100% organic production in three to five years.

The Cuban government offers financial incentives to urbanites who agree to move to the countryside to provide the increased labor necessary for organic agriculture. The increased need for rural labor has huge implications for stemming the massive rural to urban migration in the developing world today which is causing metropolitan areas to swell and be overcome with squalid migrant communities.

There are countless benefits to organic foods. Not only are pesticide and herbicide residues significantly lower in organic foods, but there are zero GMOs used in organic cultivation. There has also been shown to be no increased risk of food poisoning in organic food (15). One study showed that organic strawberries, blackberries and corn contained more antioxidants such as vitamin C and E than their conventional counterparts (16). Organic livestock do not get antibiotics in huge doses like conventional ones, so they don't contribute to the development of resistant microorganisms. Countless studies have shown the nutritional superiority of organic foods. One study done in the U.S. showed that people who have eaten an organic diet excrete flavinoids and show signs of antioxidant activity. That is, they have more anti-oxidants in their system (17). One pro-organic author, in commenting on depleted conventionally-produced foods, states "Given that most Americans eat conventionally-produced food, the diminished vitamin and mineral content of this food could lead to long-term nutritional inferiority and adverse health effects" (18). Organic crops also show lower levels of nitrates and heavy metals (19). In a study that investigated 41 previous nutritional studies published in the Journal of Alternative and Complimentary Medicine, organic crops were shown to contain substantially more Vitamin C, iron, magnesium, phosphorous, and useable protein (20).

There are several encouraging indices of the growth and increased acceptability of organic food. In 2000, more organic food was sold in mainstream supermarkets than in natural-food stores, marking its movement into mainstream consumption. Also, the Organic Foods Act of 1990 established the first organic farming certification standards in the United States, and the USDA itself nationalized these standards in 2002.

Studies have also been done on the profitability of organic agriculture as compared to its conventional counterpart. The most common consensus is that chemical farming is more profitable in the short term, while organic farming is overwhelmingly so in the middle and long term. Although organic farms are slightly less profitable immediately, this is offset by the decreased cost of inputs. Moreover, when natural resource depletion is calculated into the economic viability equation, organic farming in the United States is predicted to compete with or exceed conventional farming (21). In a study done in France in 2000, it was found that organic farms were often just as profitable as conventional ones, especially in the long run. And although the crop rotation and diversity of an organic system lessens the total land available for cash crops, this diversification proves very beneficial for the health and balance of the local economy as well as of local denizens (22).

It is very common for as much as three-fourths of a developing nation's populations to be employed in rural agriculture, yet with the recent surge of conventional farming and the ensuing soil loss and local environmental pollution, many countrysides are now proving unable to support high rural populations. Due to this pervasive fact, organic agriculture, on an individual and organizational level, is being expanded, implemented, and accepted as the best direction for growth and regeneration of the environment and of agricultural yields. This is a relatively easy fit for many underdeveloped nations because organic or low-input farming is essentially synonymous with traditional centuries-old local farming techniques. Most of the support for such a shift is being given by non-governmental organizations from the developed world, yet some national governments are offering aid and financial encouragements. Cuba is an excellent example of this, as is the Latin American region in general. Europe displays the greatest degree of governmental involvement in the shift to organic. Sizeable financial incentives are offered to farmers who shift to sustainable agriculture, and some public institutions like schools and hospitals are encouraged or required to purchase organic food (23).

In conclusion, the short-term health benefits and long-term sustainability of organic, traditional agriculture make it an increasingly attractive option for nations and regions across the world. Its adoption in the developing world has proven especially smooth, given that its main precepts of symbiosis with nature and utilization of natural pest control and fertilization jibe very well with traditional tropical agriculture. Moreover, the short-term profitability of conventional farming is gradually proving to be decidedly unprofitable in the medium and long term because the process destroys the source of its own proliferation – the soil itself. The increasing demand for organic goods in Europe and elsewhere are generating a big push for the spread and implementation of environmentally aligned, sustainable agriculture in upwards of 100 nations. Simultaneously, the wake of the last few decades of conventional farming in the first and third worlds has left many landscapes denuded and polluted to the point that crop production has been severely diminished in a time when the opposite is called for.

It is becoming apparent that organic, sustainable cultivation is not only an attractive, but now an inevitable future for global agriculture. When the agri-business giants in the United States begin to give way to the increasingly desired and more environmentally advantageous organic counterpart, this will mark a profound shift in the way we grow and consume food on this planet. Hopefully this transition will not be one of begrudged economic necessity, but rather one of conscientious, aware, and preemptive decision making on the part of industry and government leaders who have the power to incite such a change.

Kim Hak-Su, the executive Secretary of the Economic and Social Commission for Asia and the Pacific (ESCAP), made a powerful statement in April of 2002 to a group in Bangkok, Thailand. What a fortuitous condition the world would be in if we heard more world leaders concur with his statement.

"We will spare no effort to free our fellow men, women, and children from the abject and dehumanizing condition of extreme poverty, to which more than a billion of them are currently subjected. We are committed to making the right to development a reality for everyone and to freeing the entire human race from want" (24).

Recycling

Several manmade things are visible from outer space including the Great Wall of China, the Pyramids of Egypt, and the Fresh Kills landfill on the southern edge of New York City (1). That is, from a distance, what is now notable about this planet is the sheer accumulation of trash. We, in the United States, besides our many global accolades, also lead the world in the production of waste. We produce about 1.5 billion pounds of trash every day, and 460 billion pounds of trash per year (2). 30 years ago, we produced half of that amount. Approximately 70% of this refuse is simply piled up in landfills, so our landfills are filling up, while new sites for dumps are increasingly difficult to locate (3). The United States economy is based on ever-increasing production and consumption. Because of this, our populace is kept largely unaware of the effects of our consumption on the environment, including fossil-fuel burning and trash production. Yet the effects of our habits are pervasive, widespread, and increasingly hard to ignore. Author Dorothy L. Sayers said in 1942 that "A society in which consumption has to be artificially stimulated in order to keep production going is a society founded on trash and waste, and such a society is a house built upon sand" (4). This imminent crisis is turning many heads toward the option of recycling.

Approximately 95% of all refuse produced is reusable or recyclable, while only 17% of the total garbage collected, the waste stream, is currently diverted from landfills to other destinations (5). Paper and food constitute over half of the contents of trash in America. Yard trimmings contribute another 10% approximately, while glass, metals, and plastics comprise another 25%. Items such as wood, textiles, and rubber account for most of the remainder. Initial recycling efforts have focused on collecting and recycling paper, glass, aluminum, and plastics. Approximately 15-20 % of the "waste stream" is recycled currently, with the number of municipal curbside recycling programs skyrocketing in the past twenty years, from 1,050 in 1988 to close to 10,000 in 2006 (6). In 1989, California's Integrated Waste Management Board (IMWB) mandated that by 2000, all municipalities needed to achieve a 50% recycled rate of all municipal solid waste (MSW) produced. Many other states instigated required recycling programs, most with notable success.

There were many immediate results from this mandate in California. First, with municipal support, countless programs were instigated on the local level. The city of Thousand Oaks, California, for instance, reported a diversion rate of 66% in 1999 (waste recycled or diverted from landfills), which amounted to 153,000 tons of material (7). The city instigated the county's largest curbside recycling program. Commercial recycling programs in the city netted another 1700 tons of recyclables. One electronics recycling day tallied 26,000 pounds of electronic equipment in one day (8).

The state of New Jersey has a mandatory recycling act which required a 90% recycled rate of solid waste by 1995. It was initiated in 1987 and three years later they had already reached a 46% recycled rate (9). The state now leads the U.S. in recycling and is an excellent example of how a cohesive statewide program can have rapid and substantial effects. Utility Plastics Recycling, Inc. in Brooklyn NY combines recyclable plastic collection and recovery with the manufacture of plastic products in one building, which does away with many economic dis-incentives to the process of transforming recyclables into reusable products. New York City has required residential recycling since 1989. This includes public education and legal enforcement of recycling mandates.

The majority of municipalities in the country have funds and programs focused on sponsoring and condoning recycling programs. Non-governmental organizations, locally and nationally, provide substantial amounts of support, education, and loans to cities who propose to further their recycling efforts. The California Integrated Waste Management Board (IWMB) publishes a resource guide for businesses interested in recycling or buying recycled products. It is an incredibly thorough guide which offers grants, loans, and other financial incentives from several major U.S. governmental organizations such as the department of energy, the EPA, Housing and Urban Development, etc. The State Water Resources Control Board offers as much as $50 million in loans for wastewater treatment and recycling as well as "non-point source" pollution projects (10).

Besides the standard recyclables such as glass, paper, and aluminum, specific programs for selected portions of the MSW stream are more and more prevalent as cities are beginning to understand the appropriate collection processes and respective destinations for their different recyclables. The major categories of these recyclables are food waste, yard trimmings, and bulky items such as appliances and furniture.

Organic materials – principally food, yard trimmings, and wood – comprise about 25% of all Municipal Solid Waste (MSW) in the U.S. today. That totals about 40 million tons of yard trimmings and 16 million tons of food that is thrown away each year. Traditionally these materials have been deposited into landfills along with other "trash." But it was discovered that in landfills these materials generate methane gas, which is harmful to the ozone layer, and toxic leachate, which invades and pollutes local groundwater. Many efforts were made to redirect the flow of these organic materials away from landfills and to beneficial destinations. One simple solution has been to isolate organic materials from the waste stream and burn the methane gas that they generate for heat energy. This process is termed "biomass utilization." Another method of organics recycling is composting. This includes "vermi-composting," or worm farms that rapidly transform organic materials into compounds utilizable as fertilizer. Vermi-compost farms are found on a large scale in only a few locations in the U.S., but on a grand scale, incidentally, in Cuba. Also used are centralized composting facilities, which are usually implemented on a community-wide basis and are most popular in the San Francisco Bay area. Last are backyard composting programs, which are present currently in half of all U.S. states. The approximately 3,000 composting programs/facilities in the country today generally include education, promotion, funding, and bin distribution (11). In some cases, un-composted yard trimmings are applied directly to agricultural fields to avert the cost of centralized composting.

Besides methane utilization and composting, there has also been an historical and recent push for conserving and distributing "waste" food before it is thrown away. Many institutions such as churches, the Salvation Army, or other non-governmental organizations have a long tradition of food drives where people donate unused canned foods, especially around the holidays. Today, these efforts have expanded due to companies like America's Second Harvest, which is a network of 200 food banks across the country that passed out one billion pounds of food in 2001 (12). The loss of resources is particularly clear and present in the case of wasted food since in California alone, 1.3 million residents were hungry in 1998, yet about four million tons of food is thrown away in the state each year (13).

Recycling of bulky products has become a part of many municipal offerings of late as well. The "Last Chance Mercantile" is a collection center where furniture, housewares, and hardware/electrical goods are offered for sale before they enter the landfill. Berkeley and Monterey, California currently support such programs. The program in Monterey, as of ten years ago when statistics were diligently collected, was grossing over $200,000 in revenue each year from the sale of discarded items. (14) The Berkeley program, called Urban Ore, grosses over $1.5 million annually. This revenue is another example of the conversion of recyclables into utilizable energy or value.

Waste to Energy (WTE) is another effective way to glean energy from the waste stream. In this process, organic and other materials are incinerated, which has been done for hundreds of years as a method of refuse disposal. Yet in WTE, the heat energy that is produced from the burning is transformed into electricity. Gauged on emissions produced for each unit of electricity generated, WTE generates less emissions than coal plants and equal or less than natural gas plants (15). By combining Biomass Utilization and Waste to Energy programs, it is conceivable that a community's waste stream may soon be a substantial contributor to its electricity consumption needs.

An important part of the waste stream/recycling puzzle is the fact that a majority of the waste that enters our national and municipal waste streams is produced by corporate and industrial sources. Because of this, recycling education and funding has been increasingly focused in these sectors in recent years in order both to increase recycling and to reduce the production of waste at the source. There are several institutions, governmental and otherwise, which offer financial incentives to commercial entities who show efforts to

The Way of the World

recycle and reduce source output. For example, the Alameda County Source Reduction and Recycling Board Revolving Loan Fund (RLF), has offered 23 loans since 1993 totaling over 2.5 million dollars (16). Loans are often also given throughout California for companies to develop their practices and facilities for diverting waste from landfills. This program is called the Recycling Market Development Revolving Loan Program, which provides low interest loans of up to $2 million to such companies (17).

Apart from funding from outside sources, there are many market-based incentives for corporations to reduce waste and increase recycling. First, increased efficiency and less waste translates to reduced operating costs. Second, fewer toxins used in production means improved worker safety and health. Third, cleaner facilities and less waste means reduced environmental compliance costs, and fourth, companies may expect to enjoy enhanced consumer acceptance due to the company's image as an environmentally aware corporation (18). Moreover, the E.P.A. estimates that containers and packaging comprised 29.7% of the total MSW in the United States in 1996. Reduction in packaging size and bulk was championed as a cause voluntarily by a company called The James River Corporation, who evaluated packaging production facilities and made helpful suggestions to several companies across the country. One manufacturer's box, upon assessment, had two inches cut off of one flap, which saved the company $360,000 at a single plant (19).

The benefits of recycling and reducing waste are myriad. The environmental benefits are manifest: it is very plausible to envision a 50% reduction in total solid waste ending up in landfills within the next decade in countless municipalities and several states (CA and NJ currently). Also, the reuse of metals, glass, plastics, and paper saves the extraction of millions of tons of virgin materials each year. Companies who increase efficiency and recycling while reducing waste will save money in environmental compliance costs and in less material used and wasted. Copious amounts of useable energy is garnered from recycling through the methane of biomass utilization, heat from Waste to Energy programs, and even ethanol fuel produced from agricultural waste products. These sources could become a verifiable part of this country's future energy equation. Moreover, recycling and reducing waste is simply financially wise. In a household or a major corporation, lowering initial costs by reducing waste saves money. While as a community and nation, putting forth a small amount of effort to recycle and divert waste from landfills is a source of income (resale of large items and reusable materials), energy (WTE and Biomass Utilization), local soil replenishment (composting), municipal cleanliness and health (less trash ending up in landfills), and community cohesion and self-sufficiency.

When more and more of these programs are implemented in various communities, we begin to see that there is very little that we throw away that cannot be reused or utilized further in some way. Many Native American tribes, the first inhabitants of this territory, gave us an excellent example of how to live in harmony with nature by only taking what they needed from nature, and using all that they took. Every part of the buffalo was used, from the fur to the meat to the sinew and tendons. That shows a respect for and understanding of the environment. We have much larger populations to support today, so that kind of idealistic synergy may not be as plausible, yet simple awareness and a conscientious effort to waste less and reuse more would make significant changes. We can also learn from nature itself, where all minerals, organic materials, water, and air on Earth have been recycled over and over for billions of years. The waste of one process – humans breathing in oxygen and exhaling carbon dioxide – becomes the building blocks of another process – plants taking in carbon dioxide and giving off oxygen. The same recycling process is evident in the cosmos with the life cycle of galaxies and stars.

Overall, politicians and business people must begin to look at recycling from a broader perspective. Financial concerns dominate any discussion of society-wide change in this country, and the American economy is based on unbridled consumption, and necessarily, upon waste. Americans are removed from an awareness of the effects of their consumptive habits, such as landfill proliferation and global warming due to fossil fuel burning. This is because this awareness would make us temper our buying and consuming habits, which would slow our economic machine. Yet this somewhat short-sighted view must begin to expand beyond money.

"While recycling is not always profitable in the short term, it is nonetheless a valid response to a long term environmental problem, which cannot be reduced to narrowly economic terms" (20). When we look at the health and prosperity of our society as a whole, allowing the capitalist profit motive to always determine our social direction and momentum has proven to be deleterious. Much more logical and realistic is a holistic, inclusive approach to our human evolution which includes long-term symbiosis with the earth and with each other. The oil and agribusiness industries are currently strongly affiliated with and/or heavily subsidized by our federal government. This affords these industries great success and productivity. Yet how would they fare without such massive help and partnership with the government? Moreover, said industries have decades of proven environmental damage on their scorecard and are showing few signs of change.

If our business leaders and political decision makers could step beyond the everyday battles of assuaging certain powerful groups, keeping economic indicators favorable, and protecting their re-election, and could glimpse the long-term trajectory of our economy, environment, and individual health, it is undeniable that at least a spark of awareness would incite some change. If the beneficial trend of recycling, along with the related trends of solar power and organic agriculture, for instance, were supported, subsidized, and advocated by an entity as mighty as the U.S. government, they would undoubtedly flourish. This would require a strong push away from the patterned lure of a predominantly economic, short term, and oligarchical basis for our national-level decisions. It would also help to promote a trust in and wholehearted embracing of policies that are the best for all involved, and whose benefits to our society will only increase as time goes on. A giant shift would then occur because our government would be supporting practices that are holistic, synergized with nature, and sustainable long into the future. This is wise husbandry of our resources. This is conscious foresight. Conscientiously managing our earth's resources by adopting a recycling lifestyle on a national scale is exactly the kind of leadership that the world today so explicitly needs, and we in the United States and as the United States are the ones called upon to provide it.

Negative Global Energies

Myopia, fear, and disregard by the hegemon, ignorance and indulgence by the West's citizenry, and a palpable pressure and desperation in the developing world are the principal negative attitudes and energies present on the globe today.

The hegemon – essentially an elite economic and political oligarchy in the richest nations in the world, but principally the U.S. – is very fearful that it will lose the power, control and resources that it now commands. This produces in it a need for domination of other cultures, and also a greed and myopia that preclude an understanding of how their actions are egregiously damaging the environment and the less fortunate peoples of the earth. These attitudes are the source of the systematic and deliberate actions taken by the hegemon and they are directly or indirectly the cause of the negative energies and practices observable in the West's citizenry and in the developing world.

One vivid example of the hegemon's desire to dominate and acquire ever more is in its suppression of third world environments, economies, and people. A surreptitious but powerful expression of this is the existence of the World Bank, which is centered and controlled on the U.S. eastern seaboard. This institution, and others like it such as the International Monetary Fund, offer loans to the developing world, yet with heavy contingencies. These so-called "structural adjustments" mandate that receiving nations open up their markets to vastly cheaper products from Western corporations, which makes domestic businesses and industries both unable to compete and vulnerable to foreign purchase. This is depleting and often devastating to these fragile economies. Also, it restricts these nations' evolution to the final stage of the "demographic transition" wherein economies can fully industrialize and fully develop allowing their population growth rates to subside. So, under these economically repressive practices, these countries have skyrocketing populations coupled with beleaguered economies. This, not surprisingly, produces a palpable desperation, which is the dominant energy of the developing world.

This desperation amidst limited options for income in the developing world has led to literally hundreds of millions of people exercising one of the few options that they have left – to sell nature. Nature, in this case, takes many forms. As a part of the commodifiable natural environment, people's bodies themselves are put up for sale on the international labor and sex trades. Logging and the sale of lumber, or deforestation, is another commodification of nature in the absence of other avenues for income. Even beautiful scenery is for sale and often abused through the tourism industry. This "nature for sale" degrades nature on many levels in the third world and its residents are left to deal with the consequences. Attitudes of myopia and domination push the hegemon to further participate in this situation by deforesting large tracts of land for cash crop plantations, scarring the earth with vast gold, diamond and mineral mines, and exploiting impoverished regions with the construction of slave-wage factories.

The hegemon subjugates its own citizenry and national purse, as well, for its individual goals. That is, it dominates its own people. Tax money is used for war, which allows for military occupation and domination of nations with desirable resources, such as oil or the flow of drugs. Tax money is also shifted within the political/economic hegemon from government to big business in the form of subsidies and tax breaks.

An ignorant and consumptive Western populace is also a critical aspect in this malevolent global equation. Ignorance is fostered both by a carefully-controlled flow of information, and by a society deluged with distraction. First, information presented through the media is significantly filtered by moneyed lobby groups. These groups, who represent the national government/big business conglomerate, put heavy pressure on networks not to broadcast information that may cast the hegemon's political and economic actions in a negative light. Along with a long-standing national self-centeredness, this censorship keeps the American population profoundly isolated from the larger realities of the globe and dependent on a manipulatable media to construct their world view. Also contributing to our myopia is distraction in the form of entertainment and fear. Over-stimulation and entertainment – from 400 cable channels and interactive voting-based TV shows to internet surfing and our daily coffee fix – together with the constant vague fear of a terrorist attack distract us very effectively from cultivating a global awareness.

A myopic populace that consumes without limit is very beneficial to the capitalist economic machine, and so it is critical that we are not made aware of the negative environmental effects of our consumption. Remote landfills, obscuring the one billion tons of refuse that we in the U.S. produce annually, are one example. Unmitigated consumption of gasoline, in particular, is fostered through a proliferation of automobile ads and an insidious and conspicuous lack of media coverage about the effects of burning fossil fuels on the environment and in producing global warming.

Avarice and disregard for the environment in the West produces rampant fossil fuel burning, waste production, and denuding of natural environments. This co-mingles with population pressure and desperation, inducing deforestation in the developing world. These dark emotions of avarice, disregard, and desperation do not generate situations or feelings of ease and health. They could be said to produce feelings of dis-ease. And their combined effect on the natural environment – producing carbon dioxide, depleting the ozone layer, and removing trees, our source of oxygen – is generating a dis-ease that is killing the earth: global warming.

Likewise, the pressure and desperation to survive in the developing world forces millions to disregard their own bodies and enter the sex trade. While ignorance, indulgence, and a fostered disregard for "the other" allow the West to patronize the international sex trade. Moreover, a broad umbrella of sexual repression in most of the world – the Puritanical foundation of the U.S., and female circumcision and general suppression of female sexuality in Africa and the Middle East – add to this dark cocktail of unease or dis-ease with sexuality on a global scale. The physical manifestation of this sully mix of emotional dis-ease with sex is the appearance and global expansion of AIDS, a sexual dis-ease. The proliferation of our dis-ease with our bodies and our dis-ease with and mistreatment of nature are hence taking form as a disease of the body – AIDS – and a disease of the Earth – Global Warming.

Without an analysis of the source of these global-scale ailments, solving them has proven difficult and delayed. These "diseases" are not accidents, nor have they come from nowhere. They are the long-developed accumulation and materialization of attitudes and circumstances that we ourselves have chosen and propagated. When our fear of a lack of power, money, resources and land subsides, and when we achieve an increased awareness of our planet, and of the injustices that we commit against the environment and each other, this shroud over our planet of fear, mistreatment and disease can be pulled back to let in the light of day. In this way, these problems can begin to be solved and healed.

Dependence on Oil

The fostering of demand, an apparently limitless supply by design, and the insidious suppression of environmental truths and awareness.

"When our excavation of oil dries up, where do we go – natural gas, solar, hydroelectric?"
"No, we just dig deeper." (1)

Dependence on oil is a very powerful and astonishingly pervasive tool. Those who control the resource of oil – an oil company/US governmental oligarchy conglomerate – utilize this dependence very effectively to ensure their continued wealth and dominance. They generate this dependence through several specific mechanisms, including: ensuring ample supply, fostering demand and consumption, suppressing awareness of environmental crises, and sabotaging information and industrial ventures of alternative energy and transport. The engendering of this dependence among oil powers and first world political oligarchies, namely in the United States, is sourced in attitudes of greed for disproportionate wealth at the expense of others, and a myopic disregard for the planet's environment.

Their most essential mechanism is securing an ample supply of oil. The goal is to create a carefree feeling among the American populace, the greatest oil market in the world, so that consumption will never be restricted. This attitude displays disregard for the environment and an immeasurable greed, since we are already the wealthiest country on earth. Yet a small cabal of government and oil officials choose to get even richer by fortifying this country's addiction to one of the most environmentally harmful substances known to man.

Due to the fact that part of the conflict in World War II was over oil, and oil embargoes to Axis powers were critical in their defeat, the United States realized the importance of a steady supply of oil to its livelihood. To that end, the U.S. took two landmark geopolitical actions. Immediately following World War II, the Bretton Woods agreement was signed in New Hampshire in 1944, which established the International Monetary Fund and the World Bank (2). Located inside the United State, these institutions use their considerable financial leverage to grant Western businesses access to third world economies and resources. Then, in 1945, President Franklin D. Roosevelt met with King Abdul Asiz ibn Saud of Saudi Arabia to set up an oil-for-protection arrangement that was and still is the foundation of the U.S./Saudi relationship (3). These two mechanisms were powerful assurance of the future access to and availability of oil for the US.

Today, the pressure to discover new sources of oil is much greater. Between 2000 and 2020, U.S. oil production will fall from 8.5 million barrels per day to 7 million barrels, yet consumption will increase from 11 million barrels to 18.5 million barrels. Therefore, by 2020, the US will need to import twice as much fuel per year as it did in 1990. In order to perpetuate the idea of limitless supply, the Bush government has the task of actively and aggressively acquiring larger and more varied sources of oil. Our most common and effective means for achieving this is military invasion and occupation.

In the year 2000, an oil pipeline had been conceived of to pass from the oil-rich Caspian sea through Afghanistan, and to the ports of Pakistan for transport. Yet the Taliban leadership of Afghanistan, former associates of the Bush Sr. administration, were not amenable to this pipeline plan. Also, Iraq's third largest oil reserves on earth were despotically guarded by Saddam Hussein, a former operative of the CIA, which was headed by Bush Sr. at the time. These were identified as huge potential new sources of petroleum, and all that was needed was an "entrance strategy" into these countries.

A few months before September 11, 2001, a briefing to Dick Cheney and George Bush read:

"Based on a review of all sources reporting over the last five months, we believe that UBL will launch a significant terrorist attack against the US and/or Israel's interests in the coming weeks. The attack will be spectacular and designed to inflict mass casualties against US facilities or interests. Attack preparations have been made. Attack will occur with little or no warning" (4).

Two months later 9/11 occurred, and soon after, the U.S. military entered Afghanistan, and several events immediately ensued which had nothing to do with terrorism and everything to do with oil acquisition in the Caspian region. First, the Pakistani oil minister met with former US ambassador to Pakistan, Wendy Chamberlin, about a proposed pipeline from the Caspian Sea to Pakistan. This pipeline passed through Afghanistan. Then, Taliban-occupied Kabul fell to U.S. military. In December, new Afghan president, Karzai, was sworn in as president and received $50 million from the White House and $100 million from the IMF for the construction of a pipeline maintenance road. Soon after, Karzi spoke with Pakistani officials about putting the pipeline into effect. Mission oil acquisition in Afghanistan accomplished. The next target was Iraq.

Having its sights set on Iraq's oil for some time, the Bush/Cheney team had been attempting to link Iraq to 9/11 for several months, and to justify a future invasion. On November 8, 2002, Resolution 1441 was passed by the UN Security Council which stated that "Iraq will face serious consequences (since they have not) provided an accurate, full, final, and complete disclosure ... of all aspects of its progress to develop weapons of mass destruction" (5). This resolution was spearheaded and heavily backed by the U.S. and the U.K. Then, several comments by White House officials began to link 9/11 to Iraq including a statement by Dick Cheney on National Public Radio in January, 2003:

"There's overwhelming evidence (that) there was a connection between Al Qaeda and the Iraq government" (6).

No such evidence was ever provided. If any more clarification was needed on the White House's intentions concerning this matter, they were disclosed by the final report of the National Commission on Terrorist Attacks on the United States, also known as the 9/11 Commission. It stated that specific members of the Bush administration deliberately used 9/11 as justification to invade Iraq (7). 9/11 was a terrible tragedy in the history of our nation's people, yet interestingly, it proved to be quite helpful to our oil/government oligarchy's continuing quest for marketable energy.

Another mechanism used by the oil power/US oligarchy to ensure dependence on oil is the suppression of awareness of the environmental crisis. This suppression of the truth is an integral and ubiquitous tool of the oil/US government conglomerate. If the public knew how devastating this oil consumption was to the environment, and the insidious lengths that our government goes to in order to secure it, massive changes would occur in consumption of oil and in the public approval of this administration. The natural result is a palpable fear in the government/oil oligarchy of being found out, and/ or toppled as an empire. Therefore, this regime is one of the most skilled political regimes of the 20th century at censorship, non-disclosure, and bending of obvious truths.

To begin, due to myriad factors including a devotion to "journalistic balance," difficulty deciphering confusing meteorological and scientific jargon, and covert pressure from oil powers, U.S. media has become a virtual accomplice to oil industry public relations groups in suppressing the connection between fossil fuel burning and global warming (8).

"We did make the link to global warming once," said one TV news editor, "but it triggered a barrage of complaints from the Global Climate Coalition to our top network executives" (The GCC was the oil and coal lobbying group) (9). The absence of this link leaves a critical gap which is elucidated by authors Maxwell and Jules Bykoff:

"Since the general public garners most of its knowledge about science from the mass media... the disjuncture between scientific discourse and popular discourse (is responsible for the fact that) significant and concerted international action has not been taken to curb practices that contribute to global warming (10).

This suppression goes past the media and into the realm of government. According to the EPA, in 2003, the agency's report on the environmental effects of climate change on the US had four paragraphs removed after the White House had access to it (11). Also, by 2003, ExxonMobil was giving more than $1 million a year to an array of ideological, right-wing organizations opposing action on climate change, including the Competitive Enterprise Institute, and Frontiers of Freedom (12).

Beyond subterfuge and hiding of the facts, there is also simple open denouncement of environmentalism and conservation. At an Associated Press meeting in Toronto in April of 2001, Dick Cheney belittled the suggestion that "we could simply conserve or ration our way out" of an energy crisis. "Conservation may be a sign of personal virtue, but it is not a sufficient basis for a sound, comprehensive energy policy (13).

These are only glimpses of the suppression of environmental awareness by the government and media. When necessary, suppression of facts is utilized, but on the global scale, a brash indifference to the environment in general is the tool. For example, in the late 90s Holland, Germany, and Britain agreed to cut their emissions by 50 to 80 percent over the next fifty years, and China has cut emissions by 19 percent even while showing 36 percent economic growth over the same period (14). During this same span of time, the U.S. offered a significantly smaller reduction in emissions than its European counterparts and also twice pulled out of the Kyoto environmental protocols (15). The greed for money, craving for oil, and fear of competition that our government exhibits are producing insidious, deleterious, and pervasive environmental damage on this earth. The power of this greed has produced a myopia that simply does not allow those in power to see that the effects of their actions are threatening the very survival of the human race. Only with a myopia this intense could this deluge of environmentally harmful practices continue.

There is also active sabotage over the last 50 years of solar and alternative transport technology by the oil power/U.S. government oligarchy. Solar technology companies who show any potential for success are often bought out by no-name businesses and then totally shut down. It seems unlikely that this would happen so often, since there would be no economic incentive, if it were not the oil powers behind these actions. Also, in the late 1950s in the Los Angeles metropolitan area, a conglomerate of three major oil companies bought out the city's largest electric light-rail system. Named the Pacific Electric, this was an incredibly extensive network of railways extending sixty miles inland and along approximately 70 miles of urban development on the coast. It was bought out and totally dismantled by 1961, and the largest urban car center on earth was born. There are now 15 million cars in Southern California, which is more than the total in any foreign country on Earth.

Solar power is insidiously described as "too expensive" and "impractical" by oil industry spokespeople. Yet some simple facts discredit this. Solar has a one-time set up cost, it is emission free, there is little or no required maintenance on solar-receiving apparatus, sunshine is virtually ubiquitous, and there is a limitless supply of solar energy forever. Oil, on the contrary, is very expensive to look for and find, using satellite imagery, magnetic resonance technology, and much manpower. Drilling apparatus and operation is costly financially and energetically. And oil is very costly and environmentally harmful to transport due to constant spillages. In fact, the equivalent of ten Exxon Valdez crashes and spillages of oil occurs every year on the Earth (16). This is a catastrophic amount of oil spilled into ocean ecological systems and this topic is conspicuously absent from news programming.

The final mechanism to be discussed is the fostering of demand. First, as already stated, there is virtually no mention of "conservation" in the media or in any public government statement. It is not that it is denounced, but that it is simply never mentioned. Conservation is the biggest enemy of the commercial oil machine, while ignorant, unmitigated consumption is its greatest ally.

In the last 50 years, "conservation" has been essentially absent from the American vocabulary. Consumption is a foundational ethos of this country and it is fed into by both the government/oil oligarchy and our capitalistic foundation.

The Way of the World

Ubiquitous automobile ads and a proliferation of gas-guzzling SUVs are testament to our unbridled enjoyment of and carefree indulgence in the delights of fossil fuels. There is a powerful affinity between the American identity and our automobiles. This is one of the greatest marketing tools for oil consumption, because while we are focused on how our car expresses who we are, the oil/U.S. government conglomerate has already won its victory in that you are driving at all.

This abundance of oil is represented powerfully and visually by the stunning ubiquity of gas stations in every urban area in the United States. The perception of a limitless supply is critical to the escalation of demand. Gas stations are located on the corners of every major intersection in modern American cities. Their vast horizontal space for pulling out of the hubbub of urban driving is a tantalizing oasis in dense urban areas. With the advent of AM/PM mini-markets, which are often open 24 hours, gas stations now provide not only gasoline, but food, public phones, restrooms, and even basic household supplies. Ubiquitous car ads marketing the automobile as the ultimate visceral and voyeuristic expression of our identity and the instilling of an unquenchable desire for ever-increasing horsepower, have made unbridled fossil fuel consumption in this culture a given. The observable prevalence of gas stations only adds to the accessibility and ease of this addiction. In summation, the current oil/governmental conglomerate goes to great lengths to ensure an ample supply of oil, to foster its demand, and to suppress any link between fossil fuel burning and global warming. New, clean, renewable energy technologies are also actively suppressed. The result, very simply, is that this country is dependent on oil, by design.

The So-Called "Drug War"

The drug war in Latin America has received much attention in the past three decades because it involves the flow of billions of dollars, principally between the U.S and Colombia. The United States government has entered this arena to a significant degree through substantial financial and military involvement. Particularly since the beginning of US "intervention," it is increasingly difficult to determine what's going on below the surface of rhetoric, distracting and disorienting activities, and shifting alliances in this hotbed of money and multi-directional conflict.

The stated goals of the United States in the drug war in Latin America are to cultivate democracy, support human rights, and curb the production of cocaine and other drugs at the source. Its principal method of achieving these goals, that is, essentially the unilateral observable action taken by our government in this arena, has been the militarization of Latin America through what are called U.S. Security Assistance Programs. These programs include four basic elements: direct monetary funding for national militaries, supply of military technology and equipment, military training by the U.S. military, and strategic advice from the United States.

Immediately there seems to be a contradiction between the humanitarian, benevolent publicly-stated goals of the government, and the aggressive, totally military-focused approach that is actually being taken. In a war of such inherent

The Way of the World

deception and clandestine motives, it is often more fruitful to look at the tangible results of an "intervention" such as this rather than trying to sift through rhetoric for some solid truth.

Taking this approach, there are four main results that are consistently seen as a result of the U.S. Security Assistance Programs. First, countries in the region are destabilized because the expanded national militaries check and surpass the power of national governments. There are frequent assassinations of anti-drug politicians, and martial (military) law is often imposed in times of "emergency." This chronology in the country of Colombia, the center of the drug trade, shows a strong correlation between U.S. involvement, militarization, and the promotion of the drug trade.

In 1982, President Belisario Betancur is elected, and in 1983 he rejects the U.S. supported extradition treaty (to oust drug czars from the country). In following, the U.S. imposes heavy economic sanctions on Colombia – mainly flowers, perishable goods, and the airlines were affected (1). In 1984, in response to "guerilla activity," Colombian military places the country in a state of siege legislatively, which greatly expands military and police power (reminiscent of the post 9/11 Patriot Act) (2). During this U.S.-led military reign of the country, in April, 1984 Justice Minister Rodrigo Lara, outspoken anti-drug critic, is assassinated. In 1989 U.S. Secretary of Defense stated publicly that finding and eradicating production and transport of drugs was a "high-priority national security mission" (3). In the same year, Luis Carlos Galan, anti-drug presidential candidate is assassinated. Then, the new elected president instituted the U.S. desired extradition policy, militarization of the drug war increased substantially, and the new president signed the Decree Law of 1859, "which empowered armed forces to arrest and hold suspects incommunicado for up to seven days in military installations" (4). This string of events is disorienting, yet what is clear is that there is a steady increase in militarization and violence, and in the midst of the U.S.'s heightened control and influence in the country through this military conduit, it is very dangerous for any member of the government to be openly against the drug trade or to openly counteract any suggestion from the U.S. government.

The second observable result of the involvement by the U.S. in the region through its security assistance programs is the prevalence of human rights abuses. Specifically, U.S.-trained Latin American military are consistently high human rights abusers. In the words of Jimmy Carter, "The outcome of such training has made Latin American military less human, less professional, and increasingly focused on civilian (non-military) affairs" (5). In Mexico and Bolivia, the areas where U.S. sponsored local military anti-drug efforts are greatest, reported human rights violations are also at their highest.

Also a product of the U.S. presence is, simply, indiscriminate military expansion and activity, often irrespective of any specific or clear goal. The Colombian government was supplied with 12 Cobra helicopters by the U.S. military, and in the words of author Eugene Bouley, Jr., "the bottom line is that the law permits the use of such weapons only for counter-narcotics operations, but increasingly U.S. representatives, both military and civilian, nod and wink when weapons are used against guerillas and other civilians" (6). Also, in attempts to fight leftist guerillas, U.S. sponsored militaries often join with drug cartel paramilitary groups in attacking and opposing guerillas. This barrage of military activity is very disorienting to any lay person who cares to investigate, and so motives, true effective actions, and real progress are extremely difficult to determine. It seems as though hyper-active military presence is one of the goals itself. It is a very effective distraction while also being a mode of implementation and presence of American force to accomplish any desired goal in the region, ameliatory or otherwise. It is interesting that U.S. sponsored forces intermittently joining with drug cartel forces is not apparently met with any disapproval by the U.S.

The fourth result of our involvement in the war is that there has been a steady increase in the supply of drugs since the early 1980s when our presence began in earnest in Colombia. This is ascertainable through CIA and UN estimates of how much money is flowing back to Colombia from the U.S. on an annual basis, which has been fairly consistent or expanding in the past two decades. Further evidence of increased supply is the decrease in price of cocaine, specifically from 1980 – $55,000 per kilo to 1995 – $10,500 per kilo (7).

In looking at the tangible evidence, there begins to be a clear connection between U.S. involvement and the *promotion*, not the inhibition of the drug trade. These results do not match on any level the stated goals of the U.S. in this intervention in Latin America. If we generate new goals which seem to match more logically with the observable results of our presence in the region, the scene can take on a new clarity. The first of what could be called our "true goals" in Latin America is to create chaos, destabilization, and war. This creates fear, legitimizes military aggression, and creates a willingness by civilians and government to surrender freedoms in the name of greater perceived safety through heightened military presence and power. This, as stated above, is precisely what happened inside the borders of the U.S. as a result of 9/11, evidence of which is the Patriot Act, an ideological extension of martial law.

The second true goal is expansion of the military and military activity. This allows for control over a populace, gives those in control access to valuable natural resources (drugs or oil), and lets the military monitor money flows in the country. Also, constant and random military activity, aggressive or passive, is very distracting and desensitizes the public to the military, allowing for greater abuses and more intensive involvement.

A third true goal is the ideological separation between military and the democratic/governmental process. This is achieved by keeping a country in a constant state of "emergency" and fear of imminent attack, so that rational constitutional legalities vanish. The military is granted total license to abuse civil and human rights or the environment in order to bring about greater "safety." A high level of fear, especially of being attacked or killed by an unseen yet publicly identified force, puts individuals in a primal survival state in which the foundation of a legal, humane society (a constitution or general moral code) is essentially ineffectual. In other words, the populace is in a state of "no holds barred" and "anything goes" because of their extreme fear. And this is an ideal situation for any military wishing to have access to and control over various societal and economic entities.

The fourth mechanism of US involvement in Latin America is to disguise its motives with a façade of words and actions. This is such a common mechanism of political machines in general, but particularly this current U.S. regime, that it is simply "the way government operates," and we are quite accustomed to it. In each case our apparent magnanimity is just a crime, renamed. "Fighting terrorism" = Stealing oil. "Drug War" = Drug cultivation. "Bring them to justice" = Assassinate non-supporters. "Peace-keeping missiles" = Bombs that kill thousands of people.

Fifth is our failure by design. We purposely fail at our stated goal of stopping or diminishing the drug trade, because this allows us to prolong our presence there in order to pursue our true goals, which are to cultivate and profit from the drug trade. If it is not by design, then it is quite curious that the most powerful military in the world cannot topple

The Way of the World

some peasant coca bean farmers and drug gangs with semi-automatic rifles. If we wanted this drug war to be over, it would have been so long ago.

Lastly, our most sought-after true goal is to maintain sovereignty over the flow of money in this industry. We do so by constantly shifting our loyalties and alliances in order to take down any powerful individuals or groups in the industry and take over their portion of control and commerce. We skillfully play government officials and drug czars off each other in order to accomplish this. We oust drug czars with the help of government extradition policies, and at the same time murder uncooperative politicians with the help of drug czars. One minute a politician or drug leader is our friend, the next they are our hunted foe. This shifting of alliances has been very commonly utilized by our government for decades in myriad global situations. Other former U.S. bed buddies who have since fallen out of favor are Manuel Noriega, Saddam Hussein, and Osama Bin Laden.

After analysis of these true goals, what is occurring yet rarely publicized in Latin American drug-producing nations seems very logical: drug income in Colombia has been stabilized, the supply of cocaine has increased, and US military presence in Latin America has been amply secured.

Amidst all of this drug cultivation and efforts at drug suppression, the environment is being substantially damaged. Drug cultivation involves deforestation and subsequent topsoil erosion, pesticide pollution of the soil and surface water, and further pollution through the use of harsh chemicals for drug processing such as sulfuric acid, acetone, and kerosene. The environmental effects of the show of anti-drug tactics are equally harmful. A chemical defoliant "tebuthiuron," which is so toxic that even its manufacturer, Dow chemical, opposes its use, often renders land unable to grow crops (8). The U.S. embassy, in connection with the host country minister of the interior, makes decisions on which defoliants to use, rather than the host country minister of agriculture. This allows for abuses of this nature.

The main objective, beneath all the signs and symbols and stated and true goals in this conflict, is increased U.S. military presence. This gives us control over the area and its resources, money flows, government, and population. It seems as though our larger goal goes even far beyond profiting from the drug trade, and is focused on simply controlling the entire area for any possible future profit or benefit. Now that our military is ensconsed, and we have secured control and influence over several realms of the functioning of these societies, we can take advantage economically and politically of virtually any development in this region in the foreseeable future.

In our cultivation of fear for public manipulation, and hyper-utilization of the military at home and abroad, the United States has come to display some classic signs of a fascist state and our regime bears resemblance in philosophy and methods to those of Germany and Italy in the 1930s and 40s. A hyper-aggressive military, censorship of the media, and strong ethnocentrism have been displayed by all three societies. We also subscribe to a traditionally "masculine" national philosophy in an increasingly female and collectively-consciused world. Our so-called war on drugs is only one example of this aggressive and myopic agenda. The era of male, self-centered, violent, and aggressive international politics and relations has dominated the globe for millennia, yet in the face of significant social and environmental disasters on the globe today, it is rapidly becoming apparent that this approach no longer serves us as a planet.

Human Traffic

Trafficking in people for prostitution and forced labor is one of the fastest-growing areas of international criminal activity and one of the sites of increasing concern to the United States and to the international community. Between 800,000 and four million people are trafficked each year worldwide. Trafficking is the third largest source of profits for organized crime – third only to drugs and arms – generating $7 to $10 billion each year (1). The majority of this activity has gone on throughout Asia for the past few decades, but now there is a shift, due to increased government regulations and protection of sex workers, namely in Sri Lanka and Thailand. These activities have largely been diverted to elsewhere on the globe where cultures and economic situations are well-positioned to receive such an industry. The main sites that are receiving this new flow of sex business, and hence, demand for sex workers, are Latin America and Africa.

The phenomenon of the sex trade is actually the expression of three principal global attitudes which all overlap in their contribution to the generation and perpetuation of the sex trade. The first is the judgment and suppression of sexuality. Our repression of sex on many levels and in the majority of the world's nations limits and stifles our sexuality, so it erupts in demented perversions and tweaked expressions such as sexual violence, pedophilia, the multi-billion dollar cyber-sex industry, and the human rights-devoid international sex trade. This repression itself, ironically, generates the draw and profitability of the sex trade; since we cannot express sexuality openly or amply, there is a creation of a false sense of scarcity of sex. We believe we must search for sex, pay for it, or even use violence to get it – and yet it is something that is so abundant and intrinsically human. This is very similar to our belief in the idea of scarcity of energy and food, while unlimited solar energy awaits our use and food surpluses spoil all over the world.

The second attitudinal trend which contributes to the existence of the sex trade is the overwhelming fear among the wealthiest in the first world of losing resources and power. Coupled with the greed to acquire ever more, this fear generates the need to dominate and suppress others. This is expressed in the economic subjugation of the developing world by first-world powers. Already beleaguered developing countries receive heavily contingent loans from western lending institutions which cripple third world economies and leave residents desperate to survive. One result of this desperation is the tidal wave of both willing and unwilling participation in the sex trade. Several nations which are not subjected to this domination, such as parts of economically-depressed Eastern Europe, are also providing sex trade workers in large numbers.

The third energetic and attitudinal trend of note that helps to generate this trade in women is male chauvinism and egotism. The result is the global denigration of women and their status as second-class citizens in most countries of the world. The United Nations publishes a Gender Related Development Index (GDI) and a Gender Empowerment Measure (GEM) which are used in its annual Human Development Report to determine a country's level of gender equality. A score of 1.0 is perfect gender equality. Norway (0.94) topped the list, while Niger (0.26) was at the bottom. Many countries in Africa are in the 0.5 range, while innumerable nations are between 0.6 and 0.75 globally (2). What this translates to is that women on this planet have less access to education, positions of power, money, social status, and perhaps most of all, free expression. The sex trade, when spurred by poverty in the area, is a natural extension of this role of women as subjugated, used, and lacking power. Women's subjugation by men is paralleled by the developing world's subjugation by the West, whereas the subjugated offers their body (sex and labor) or natural fecundity (minerals and resources) to the dominant power.

Yet amidst this utter denigration of women selling their bodies, women are also simultaneously elevated in importance and power because of their dual role and dual income as laborers and sex workers. In beleaguered developed world economies, this expanded income directly sourced from the first world posits women on an entirely new level in society. Despite the source of this money, sex workers often have pride in their observably moneyed status. They become the supporter of their families, including brothers and husbands. Considering that in several destitute countries there are over a million "moneyed" female sex workers, this constitutes a gigantic shift in gender roles, and in the power of women in general.

Many women voluntarily enter the sex trade, but a huge proportion of them do so by coercion by a variety of methods including outright kidnapping and exportation to another country, lure by phony job offers in foreign countries, or false marriage opportunities with Westerners that are advertised in local papers. All of these mechanisms are used to dupe women into accepting transport to another country, where the story changes and the institution of debt bondage is enacted. The transported women are told that they owe in upwards of 30, 000 U.S. dollars for the cost of their transport, which they can pay off by working in sex bars or brothels. These women are essentially enslaved: monitored

24 hours a day and forced to acquiesce to all clients' demands. Debts are usually paid in a few to several months (3).

This debt dependence is used as a tool of the dominant, or "hegemon" throughout history and across cultures. After slavery ended in the United States, blacks in the south commonly entered into the sharecropping system in which they rented land at rates too high to pay back with crops that grew on the land, so they were perpetually in debt and subjected to the demands of the land owner. The IMF and World Bank use a very similar strategy with large loans to the developing world which allow the lending institutions to control and manipulate these economies at their will while debt dependence is still in effect. Another parallel is that in the African slave trade and the modern sex trade, the wrangling and selling of local victims to Western powers is facilitated by locals of the same tribe or ethnic group as the victim.

Governments play a crucial role in the perpetuation of this industry as well. There is a chosen myopia and active ignorance of the problem, as if governments just hope it goes away. First, there are inadequate international laws, as penalties for trafficking in humans are often minor compared to trafficking in arms or drugs.

The lack of official acknowledgement of the sex trade itself precludes the granting of official "worker" visas to sex workers. Hence they are subject to all manner of human rights violations and are not protected by local law enforcement, nor eligible for public health care.

Also, on a national scale, punishment of sex workers is much more common than punishment of traffickers. In the case of Thai migrant workers in Japan, "if employers or traffickers are prosecuted at all, they are charged with immigration offenses, the employment of illegal aliens, or with operating an unlicensed entertainment business. They are

The Way of the World

almost never prosecuted for the severe human rights abuses they have committed, such as forced labor, illegal confinement, and physical violence" (p. 6 Owed Justice, 2000). Moreover, anti-prostitution or anti-illegal immigration laws directed at the victims only exacerbate the problem by increasing the profitability of the industry. In countries where prostitution is legal, trafficking is less common and the sex industry is more regulated (5).

The Asia Migrant Bulletin has documented the trafficking of migrants from the Philippines, Thailand, China, Indonesia, Burma, Sri Lanka, Bangladesh, India, Nepal, and of late from Vietnam, Laos, Cambodia, and Fiji. They were sent to the nations of Japan, Taiwan, Hong Kong, Macao, Malaysia, Singapore, Thailand, India, Australia, Europe, and the United States (6). Yet as stated earlier, there has been a diminishment of sex trade activity in Thailand and Sri Lanka, two main centers of the trade, due to greater awareness and stronger laws in those countries. Sex commerce has shifted principally to Latin America, the Caribbean, and Africa. These newly engaged regions are susceptible and "primed" for this invasion of money and domination because of their depressed economies and also due to the strong tradition of male dominance and patrilinealism in these regions. Approximately 50,000 women from the Dominican Republic currently work abroad in the European sex industry, principally in Austria, Germany, Greece, Italy, and the Netherlands (7). The following is a quotation about poverty as a cause of sex trade activity in the Dominican Republic:

"In the case of Dominican women, the proceeds from prostitution are used to support parents or children. For those women really concerned about providing such support, opportunities in the legal economy are very limited in a society where 80 dollars a month is the minimum salary for domestic work" (8).

With an undergirding of so much repression and denouncement of sexuality imposed upon women of the world, and in sex trade regions in particular, feelings of guilt, self-denial, sacrifice, and shame are a logical experience for women selling their bodies for sex with acquaintances or strangers. Also, from the other side of this equation, guilt, disregard, and domination are the energetic foundation of the Westerners wanting to set loose their sexual desires on helpless or even coerced victims. None of the feelings and attitudes that these role players in the sex trade bring to an encounter could be described as positive, pleasant, or "healthy." And this profound feeling of dis- ease that each brings to the experience is real, and it is manifested on a large scale in the observable physical diseases associated with this sex trade, namely AIDS. The prominence and gravity of this particular disease is paralleled by the prominence and gravity of the feeling of dis-ease inside these sex trade participants.

One extreme example of this is in southern Africa, which has the highest concentration of people with AIDS on earth. In a few countries in this region, 20% or more of the adult population has the disease (9). Of note, women's rates of AIDS in the region often approach double that of men's. If we look at the extreme dis-ease with sex that women in the region have imposed upon them, the prominence of the sex-related disease of AIDS among these women is more understandable.

This energy of sexual suppression and mistreatment among African women is so extreme and visceral in Africa that it frequently results in the death of women. A woman's sexual desire is not an accepted emotion; a woman who commits adultery is often severely beaten or burned, and fiercely judged or ostracized. In situations of infidelity, the murder of a woman by her husband is often not strictly forbidden or monitored. Rape is so common that many marriages begin when the woman is raped by an acquaintance. Rape is also a tool of demoralization and power which is commonly utilized in civil wars on the continent. One cultural phenomenon in sub-Saharan Africa – female genital mutilation, or female circumcision – is a vivid and egregious example of the sexual mistreatment of women. Often at the age of eight to ten, young girls in Africa have their clitoris scraped off with blunt traditional, non-medical instruments. The procedure is called "purification" because of its effect of diminishing the woman's sexual pleasure and hence her sexual drive in order to ensure her fidelity to her husband. Approximately two million new girls each year face the prospect of female circumcision.

On the macro-commercial level, the human sex trafficking industry generates $7 to $10 billion a year for organized crime (10). A notable Thai economist has estimated that the annual income generated by Thai sex workers in Japan alone is 310,500 million yen, or U.S. $3.3 billion (11). Traffickers are from all over the world: gangs from China, Mexico, Central America, and Russia as well as Chinese and Vietnamese triads, the Japanese Yakuza, South American drug cartels, and the Italian Mafia (12).

As in the cases of drugs and arms, the United States is getting involved in this huge illicit flow of cash and product. On the surface, of course, our government's intent is purported to be benevolent, yet with a glance at the policies of the last two presidential administration's approaches to the issue, some clear variances from benevolence are detectible:

1) First, in the Bush plan, in 2002 the U.S. Attorney General announced the implementation of special "T" visas for undocumented victims of trafficking in the United States who cooperate with U.S. law enforcement officials by divulging identities of their

traffickers. They are granted permission to stay in the United States.

2) Second, in the same year, Bush signed an executive order creating an inter-agency task force to "monitor and combat trafficking in persons." This task force is heavily stocked with political and intelligence power, and it includes: the Secretary of State, the Attorney General, the Secretary of Labor, the Director of the CIA, and the Office of the National Security Advisor.

3) Third, the Department of Justice was commissioned to institute training programs for federal prosecutors, INS personnel, and FBI agents aimed at locating human traffickers.

4) In early 2003, Attorney General John Ashcroft indicated that since passage of the U.S. anti-trafficking legislation the year before, the U.S. Department of Justice has doubled the number of prosecutions and convictions for trafficking. (13).

So, looking at the Bush plan, it seems substantial, focused, and a serious call to arms against this cause. Yet when we look at the Clinton plan from a few years earlier, the excessive force, focus on punishment, and an obvious interest in finding the flow of cash in this industry becomes apparent. Clinton's plan has a totally different emphasis: one that might truly be described as benevolent.

The Clinton plan and related goals were as follows:

1) Increase economic opportunities for potential victims, increase public awareness of trafficking dangers and the entity of human trafficking in general.

2) Generate legislation to provide shelter and support services to victims who are in this country unlawfully and therefore ineligible for public assistance.

The Way of the World

(No need to disclose trafficking bosses to receive assistance from Clinton administration).
3) Press for legislation that enacts restitution for trafficked victims as a possibility through bringing private civil lawsuits against traffickers. Discover legislative ways to go after and prosecute traffickers and increase penalties that they can face (14).

The difference in the impetus and philosophy behind these two plans is monumental. Cast against the Clinton plan, the Bush administration policy's excessive force, focus on punishment, and obvious interest in finding the flow of cash in this industry become apparent. In what would normally be seen as a humanitarian extension, the Bush administration has provided over $100 million to over 100 countries to aid in the amelioration of the trafficking in women (15). Yet our hundreds of millions put into the Latin American and Southeast Asian drug trades and the copious evidence of our spurious and clandestine involvements in both locations casts our new-found interest in sex trafficking in a questionable light. Any military involvement or financial investment by our government in another country in the last century, but especially in the last ten years, is difficult to be viewed with more than reserved circumspection.

Statistics, legislation, and governmental policies related to the sex trade help to elucidate the larger problem, but a true story of a victim of sex trafficking can have a different, more human impact. The following is a real-life profile taken from Campagna and Poffenberger's *The Sexual Trafficking in Children: an investigation of the child sex trade:*

"On August 1, 1984, an older white male was arrested by police officers of New York City's 7th Precinct for sexually abusing a nine year old Mexican boy. The child, Luis, had been registered two or three days earlier at a summer day camp on New York's lower east side by the same man.

An observant youth worker noticed that Luis was depressed, crying, and walking as though in pain. She took him aside and asked what was wrong. The story, as told to investigators from Defense for Children International – USA, was that Luis was born in Acapulco, Mexico. The father of his large and very poor family was approached three weeks before by a visiting Anglo who offered to take the boy to New York, provide him with an education, teach him English, and eventually find him a job. An unknown amount of money changed hands and Luis was brought to the United States, without proper documentation, past immigration officials. The effect on Luis of such a change in environment, from sunny Acapulco to the lower east side of New York, was doubtless traumatic. He had been separated from family, friends, school, his entire way of life, only to become a victim of sexual assault" (16).

The Gift of Tragedy
Visions of a Bold and Inevitable Future for the United States

Today on this earth, 40,000 children will die of starvation. A few thousand girls will be forced into the sex trade by their families, 200,000 acres of rainforest will be cut down, and a few hundred thousand members of the US military will arise and patrol a foreign country.

Most of us in the Western world have a vague understanding of these realities but it is somehow very easy for us to continue life as usual – picking out tile for the new bathroom, rounding our triceps at the gym, watching our favorite reality TV show – all while others beseech the heavens for a bag of rice or a life-saving penicillin shot for their child.

And so sometimes we need a wake-up call to return our focus to what is essential in this life and on this earth. We've been getting them frequently of late:

9/11
The Tsunami in Asia
Hurricane Katrina

These huge and jarring events come along and they shake us to our core – for the very purpose of reminding us *of* our core – those we love, our health, and the health of our home, this planet. The messages of 9/11 and of the Tsunami, while apparent immediately, are even more clear in retrospect. 9/11 evoked the greatest show of national unity and compassion for fellow Americans that most of us have ever witnessed. It also had the potential to wake us up to some of our government's wrongdoings in the Middle East, but this realization, en masse, was not actualized. The tsunami, because its victims were locals as well as tourists from all over the world, had the amazing effect of creating an instant global consciousness. All of us were hurt, all of us were affected, all of us were helping. It was an astonishing equalizer and it provided a very effective experience of our interconnectedness. It also served to bring a flood of help and resources and Western attention onto some of the most destitute parts of the world – Indonesia and India.

Natural and human-induced disasters are an effective way for the living earth and the collective human consciousness to communicate with us as individuals. The earth is a dynamic living system which displays an amazing ability to adapt and rebalance itself after destabilizing events and eras on the globe. In this way the earth could be said to have a consciousness. Perhaps the recent substantial and documented rise in the frequency of natural disasters is the earth's way of rebalancing itself and of waking us up so that we may come into harmony with it. Human-induced disasters like 9/11 could be said to arise in a similar way, in that an unacknowledged part of the collective human consciousness has asserted itself so that we must take notice and begin to come into harmony with *it*. And so, jarring events, both human and environmental in source, arise to bring awareness to parts of humanity which are isolated or which do not perceive themselves or their actions to be affecting the larger whole.

Hurricane Katrina has jarred and affected many of us, but have we gotten the message that it has sent us? Are we still in shock and have we not yet imbibed the inherent mes-

The Way of the World

sages that the hurricane has provided? If any jarring event comes into our life and our response is only sadness or shock or anger or confusion, then we have not received the message, and another wake-up call is destined to come. She did. Her name, this time was Rita, but the message was still the same. And so, after the shock and pain subsides, we must look to the deeper messages that Katrina and Rita offer to us. Because the only reason any "tragedy" arises is so that a greater ongoing tragedy can be brought to our attention, and stopped.

The first result and message that Katrina provided was to bring our government's focus back onto home turf. Our government, for good or bad, spends perhaps a majority of its energies, money and focus on endeavors outside of this country. Fighting wars, acquiring new markets for our mega-corporations, and involving ourselves in the affairs of various nations across the globe leaves little time to focus on our own people, our own cities, our own issues. Katrina reminded us of that. Also due to Katrina, many in this country have acquired a true sympathy for those in other nations who are in catastrophic, desperate situations. It is often very easy for us to get lost in our lives of luxury, abundance and entertainment, and to passively ignore the obvious tribulations of much of the rest of the world. The hurricane gave us a visceral first-hand feeling of commonality with struggles in the developing world, in particular the millions of dislocated peoples and refugees that we see depicted on television so often. One New Orleans woman said it best when viewing images of her city in shambles, "It looks like the third world."

Another, and perhaps less major, message from Katrina was to display that in any and all situations, from coup de etats to hurricanes to bake sales, our government has one unilateral response: military presence. It appeared totally inappropriate in a scene of such tragedy, death, and despair, to inject heavily-armed national guardsmen to walk the streets with orders to shoot anyone trying to "loot" food or basic survival supplies. It seems that the only fitting response to such a tragedy would be overflowing empathy and care.

In a larger sense, and in perhaps her greatest service to us, Katrina jarred us enough to cut through our cultural insulation and myopia and wake us up both to the essentials in our own lives and to an expanded awareness of the larger human struggles on this earth – rampant starvation, a slave-like global labor trade, and rapid deforestation, for instance. If we were to take it upon ourselves to heed Katrina's call and step back and look at the world and these human struggles from that expanded awareness, that new perspective, what would we see? That is, what's going on in the world today that produces such suffering, imbalance, and separation?

The response to this evokes a list of the usual suspects: attitudes of fear and greed in the West inciting subjugation of the world's peoples, along with a myopic overconsumption and lack of global awareness. This is linked to a palpable desperation and struggle to survive in the third world, resulting in the sale of human beings and of nature itself. This mix of fear, greed, myopia, and desperation is generating a thriving sex and labor trade, fossil fuel pollution, rapid deforestation, and the ensuing corporal and terrestrial diseases that are sourced in these actions – AIDS and global warming. These are fundamental realities of our globe today which we may deliberately make ourselves aware of by removing ourselves from the mainstream media cocoon, rather than waiting for a "wake-up call" from nature or society.

But why do we continue to need such jarring wake-up calls in recent months and years? Specifically, why do we, here in America, need to be awakened? The answer is, sim-

The Way of the World

ply, that we live in isolation and virtually constant distraction. We are isolated from the world's problems physically, by two oceans, and ideologically, from the carefully-selected media images that give us a limited view of the world outside of our cultural bubble. At the same time, there is such a deluge of these selected images and information about the larger globe outside of our hamlet that our innate desire to investigate the world around us is effectively overwhelmed and we are goaded to return to the local, more manageable level. This perpetuates our isolation, as does the fact that this information is all funneled through one necessarily biased media outlet. Also, we indulge in all manner of distraction on such an extreme level because we need to voraciously fill the void in our lives as individuals and as a nation – left by a noticeable lack of purpose. Having achieved near effortless subsistence, individually, and unmatched global influence nationally, we ache for a new goal. The modern Western denizen has days filled with sound and fury, with frappucinos and business meetings and 1000 song I-pods, and yet devoid of real purpose, lacking an endeavor that truly affects the world....positively.

This lack of purpose is literally killing us. Our hearts ache in the deep inner awareness that there are so many problems on this earth, so many of us suffering, and yet we do nothing. Without a purpose, a cause, a goal that animates us and in some way affects the world, especially amidst such widespread suffering and need, our hearts are literally in disease. We are aching to be, to help, to strive, to ameliorate, to express our power – but that power, that help, that magnanimous, active being is not expressed. And each day that this goes on our soul, the heart of who we are, dies a small death. And so in this developed world, the number one killer is dis-ease of the heart: the symptom of an unengaged self, an unexpressed soul.

The pain of this emptiness, this void that is left in absence of a purpose, is killing us inside, and we try to assuage this pain and emptiness through all manner of distraction. One principal mode of distraction is fear, the main source of which is our government. When human beings experience acute fear of attack, our primal "fight or flight" response is engaged, and we become totally focused on averting immediate danger. This response to a potential threat is natural, yet when this primal response is continually activated day after day, our attention is never allowed to settle on rational daily or domestic issues. Constant and acute fear also goads us into relinquishing many of our freedoms in the name of safety.

Consumerism is also a constant and omnipresent distraction from living out our purpose. The idea that we must constantly consume all manner of entities, objects and even ideas in order to simply get through each day is a central ethos of this country. Television, consumerism's greatest tool, renders our minds numbed and defenseless as commercials manufacture demand by hawking their wares directly into our brains. Due to marketing, packaging, and advertising, a homogenization of products is created whereby the conditions, laborers, and natural materials which came together to produce an item are very effectively obscured. This keeps Western consumers insulated from an awareness of how their purchases help to perpetuate deleterious global trends. The simple act of constantly buying and consuming is a ubiquitous, powerful, and pervasive distraction in our society and it keeps us centered on our individual needs, and focused on the local, provincial, and short-term scale.

As our emptiness from lack of passion and purpose grows, so must the range and accessibility of entertainment. Each day our minds and bodies are overwhelmed by a deluge of entertainment: from Muzak on the elevator at work to 400 cable television channels, an entire apothecary of rec-

The Way of the World

reational drugs, and endless services, images, and corporal and mental stimulation – all of which dull our senses and keep our attention off any substantive national or global-level concerns. Our soul ravenously pursues expression and fulfillment, yet in the absence of true self-expression it will accept anything, and through fear, consumerism, and entertainment, we keep it distracted, numbed, over-stimulated, and yet still under-engaged.

And so in this great nation whose credo and lifeblood has always been a deep passion and purpose, an unmatched desire to be more, we now ache and writhe in the absence of a mission. We deluge our lives with distraction and entertainment but the void which craves agency and action is not filled, and we yearn for somewhere to focus our tremendous energy and unequaled efficacy. We are a racehorse that is locked in its stable, a muscle car with no road on which to roar. And in this staleness, as in the bare moments in the life of anyone or anything of greatness, we look everywhere for satisfaction, for self-expression, for fulfillment. In the absence of a real goal, our desire still spills forth, and it emerges as an insatiable desire for food, for entertainment, for products and vacations and possessions and money and titles. Excess weight from sedentary lives, stress from imbalanced focus on money and career, and diseased hearts from a lack of true connection and purpose in the world – these are our national diseases, the symptoms of our lack of substantive agency, the evidence of our stalled, aching, imploding potential.

Our government is in a similar fix. Although it has already achieved total global financial, cultural, and political supremacy, its desire for more ravenously marches it forward, vanquishing ever more cultures for resources and markets for the wild beast of capitalism. Its inner hollowness and dissatisfaction, and a desperate, constant searching in the well-traveled realms of global domination is evidenced in the diseases of its over-evolved hegemony: the deaths it causes in overseas wars, its bankrupted national purse, and the diminished quality – from lack of attention – of its domestic institutions, programs, and amenities. The government's sluggish, unimpressive response to the devastation in New Orleans is a vivid example of this.

In the past 200 years, the evolution of our national goals and collective purpose has been as follows: Independence from England…check. Manifest Destiny….check. Global hegemony…check. Totally controlling the financial, political, and cultural current of the earth….check.

And now we, as debaucherous individuals and nation – like rock stars who have had all the money and sex and drugs that a person can have – recoil at the thought that there is nothing more at the end of this line. So we push forward, into more debauchery, more entertainment, and more domination, until eventually, we spiral ourselves into demise. And this is where our government and nation is headed: exorbitantly spending, wasteful and destructive of the environment, and mortally aggressive internationally. As a people, we are overweight, hyper-medicated, overstimulated, and painfully under-engaged. We are going crazy in the trapped energy of our own potential.

We need a new, clear, real goal as a nation. We have conquered and dominated, and we have industriously expanded our economy and spread our power and influence to every reach of the globe. We have surfeited ourselves of power and conquest. What we are searching for now is something beyond that, something different, something more. We need a totally fresh direction in which to channel our considerable brain power, resources and latent energy. At the same time, a huge portion of the earth is destitute, struggling, and beleaguered. They suffer and scrape for survival in a fiercely competitive globe which leaves them consistently at the bottom. As we gradually, and sometimes poignantly wake up to our true purpose, and simultaneously to the troubling realities on this planet, we will see that our desire for purpose and the developing world's need for care, attention, and true problem-solving are perfect complements to each other. What will give us the greatest joy and satisfaction and expression of who we are is to use our ingenuity and considerable resources to actively, consistently, creatively ameliorate and aid the most beleaguered sections of the globe. And this exact response from us is precisely what the developing world desires most – to be uplifted and supported, rather than subjugated, by the entities that have the power and the choice to do either one.

This is what our individual and national soul wants most – a true purpose, a task which profoundly affects the world. In these actions and in this new way of being, a wave of fulfillment will pour over and through us that will wash away the dis-ease of a fermenting lack of purpose. A consistent dose of our help and attention would heal so much of what ills the most destitute parts of this globe on a scale that approaches the miraculous. The most refreshing new direction for us as a nation will be to give to the world what we have always given to ourselves – opportunity, the power of self-determination, and in following, prosperity and abundance. And the most healing, gratifying experience for those in need would be to know, simply, that help is on the way. What we desire as a government and a populace is renewed purpose, and that renewed purpose… is helping where we used to hurt, caring where we used to disregard, giving when we used to take. Only when you give do you realize how much you truly have. And so the biggest blessing for a country that has always craved more – is for us to give more, and in that giving, we will experience an abundance grander than any we have ever known. And so the "more" that we are looking for as a nation, and the feeling and experience that is the next stage in our advancement, is benevolence. This does not mean that we simply hand out all of our money; it refers to a state of being in which we are always looking to uplift, support, heal, and unify.

Moving into benevolence will be our last power move, our final strategy in international diplomacy and it will represent the arrival of our final stage of evolution as a nation and a people.

Virtually every powerful western society has moved through an evolution which has been based on the acquisition of money and power – from colonialism to manufacturing to technology and then to information and entertainment. Yet when a society's needs for money and power and materialism have been met many times over, and it has achieved so much individual success, money, and power that it begins to debaucherously wade in the trappings of its own grandeur, the only satisfying and effective manner in which it can advance is to move into giving and into benevolence. In this final stage, because its needs are met, a society's goals make a profound shift from an inward focus to an outward focus. Nascent expressions of benevolent societies are now observable in parts of Europe. Yet the burden and the power to change rests in our hands, because, simply, our influence over the affairs and trends on this globe is unmatched.

And for the citizens and politicians who equate benevolence with weakness and who still long for the traditional, more limited expressions of American power, what more of a power rush can there be than to be at the helm of the planet and to choose to usher the entire globe into a new level of prosperity and healthy interdependence? We have this power. And in every political and personal encounter, benevolence is always the evidence of greatest power, while attack and avarice reek of desperation and weakness.

For good or bad, we as a nation have never let anything stand in our way. We have always been a nation that thrives on seeing the tangible evidence of its power, the visible re-

The Way of the World

sults of its efficacy. Virtually never in our nation's history have we been limited, ever been defeated, ever not succeeded, surmounted, excelled. It is our national character, our nature, our essence, to succeed. I see no better choice, no country who I would trust more with the job now of saving the world than the United States. Moreover, the truth of our country, the feeling and essence laid down by our forefathers – the belief in the equality of all human beings, and of the pursuit of health, happiness, and freedom – is still the foundation of who we are – it lives in the hearts of American citizens. We have always been a home for those fleeing oppression, the haven for those in need, a beacon of light for the world.

And now, at this critical turning point in history, our political, cultural, and economic prowess and influence is unmatched. For this reason, the redirection of our national focus from individual goals to collective ones would constitute one of the greatest social and political shifts that the world has ever seen. In many ways, the destiny of the globe is in our hands. It is simply our choice in the coming years and decades whether we will aggressively expand our markets overseas and invade and suppress strategic countries, or if we will finally let go of the need for conquest and competition and instead simply, benevolently, magnanimously extend our hand, and lift up the world.

Bibliography

Global Awareness Footnotes

(1) Information Society Statistics. Data 1997-2002. European Commission, 2003.
(2) Wilson, Michele A. *Technically Together: Rethinking Community within Techno-Society.* Peter Land, 2006: 6.
(3) Crothers, Lane. *Globalization and American Popular Culture.* Rowman & Littlefield Publishers, Inc. Boulder, 2007: 60.
(4) Crothers, 2007: 58.
(5) Barber, Benjamin. *Jihad vs. McWorld: Terrorism's Challenge to Democracy.* Ballantine Books, New York. 1995.
(6) Crothers, 2007: 62.
(7) Crothers, 2007: 62.
(8) Crothers, 2007: 140.

Other Sources:

Barlow, "A Declaration of the Independence of Cyberspace" Online: http://www.eff.org/pub/publications/John.Perry.Barlow/barlow.0296.declaration. (May 2002).

Dyson, Ester. Release 2.1: *A Design for Living in the Digital Age*. London: Penguin Books. 1998.

Mattelart, Armand. *The Information Society: An Introduction*. Sage Publications. 2003.

Poster, Mark. *The Second Media Age,* Cambridge Polity Press. 1995: 24.

Preston, Paschal. *Reshaping Communications: Technology, Information and Social Change*. Sage Publications. London, 2001.

Ross, Gina. *Beyond the Trauma Vortex: The Media's Role in Healing Fear, Terror, and Violence*. North Atlantic Books. Berkeley, CA 2003.

Sky corporate "factsheet,' http://media.corporate-ir.net/media_files.Ise/bsy. Uk/factsheet.pdf. (June, 1995).

Wired 1996, 'The Wired Manifesto.' October 1996:42-7.

Solar Footnotes

(1) Kryza, Frank. *The Power of Light: The Epic Story of Man's Quest to Harness the Sun*. McGraw-Hill, 2003: XIII.
(2) Kryza, 2003.
(3) Kryza, 2003.

(4) Goetzberger, A. and V.U. Hoffmann. *Photovoltaic Solar Energy Generation.* Springer, Heidelberg. 2005.
(5) Carless, Jennifer. *Renewable Energy: a Concise Guide to Green Alternatives.* Walker and Company, New York. 1993.
(6) Carless, 1993.
(7) Bradford, Travis. *Solar Revolution: the Economic Transformation of the*
(8) *Global Energy Industry.* MIT Press, 2006.
(9) Carless, 1993.
(10) Singh, Madanjeet. *The Timeless Energy of the Sun for Life and Peace with Nature.* Unesco Publishing, 1998.
(11) Golob, Richard and Eric Brus. *The Almanac of Renewable Energy.* World Information Systems. Henry Hold Company. New York, 1993.
(12) United States Energy Institute, 2002.
(13) Bradford, 2006.
(14) "The Greenhouse Effect," Greenpeace Publications, 2002: 2-3.
(15) Bradford, 2006, and Katzman, Martin. *Solar and Wind Energy: An Economic Evaluation of Current and Future Technologies.* Rowman and Littlefield, 1984.
(16) Carless, 1993.
(17) Bradford, 2006: 8.
(18) Bradford, 2006.
(19) Kryza, 2003: 247.

Other Sources:

Beattie, Donald A. Ed. *History and Overview of Solar Heat Technologies.* MIT Press Cambridge and London, 1997.

Fanchi, John R. *Energy in the 21st Century*. World Scientific Publishing, 2005.

Halacy, D.S. Jr. *The Coming Age of Solar Energy*. Harper & Row Publishers. New York, 1963 and 1973.

Miyake, Jun, Yasuo Igarashi, and Matthias Rogner, Eds. *Biohydrogen III, Renewable Energy Systems by Biological Solar Energy Conversion*. Elsevier. Oxford, 2004.

Renewables Information: 2006. International Energy Agency. OECD/IEA, 2006.

Stanley, Tom. *Going Solar: Understanding and Using the Warmth in Sunlight*. Stonefield Publishing, 2004.

Benevolent Organizations Footnotes

(1) Union of International Association, 2004.
(2) Rodrigues, Maria Guadalupe Moog. *Global Environmentalism and Local Politics: Transnational Advocacy Networks in Brazil, Ecuador, and India*. State University of New York Press, 2004.
(3) http://nobelprize.org
(4) Miechel, Robert Cameron. "From Conservation to the Environmental Movement." *Resources for the Future*. Washington, D.C. 1985: 2.
(5) *200 NGOs in China: A Special Report from the China Development Brief*. January, 2005.
(6) Richmond, Oliver P. Ed. and Henry F. Carey. *Subcontracting Peace: The Challenges of NGO Peacebuilding*. Ashgate, 2005.

(7) Eversole, Robyn Ed. *Here to Help: NGOs Combating Poverty in Latin America.* M.E. Sharpe. New York and London, 2003
(8) Swarts, Frederick A. "NGOs and Environmental Conservation." From Hamad, Tajeldin, et al. *Culture of Responsibility and the Role of NGOs.*
(9) 200 NGOs in China, 2005.
(10) 200 NGOs in China, 2005.
(11) Hamad, Tajeldin, Frederick Swarts, and Anne Ranniste Smart, Eds. *Culture of Responsibility and the Role of NGOs.* Paragon House, 2003.
(12) Richmond, 2005.
(13) "NGOs in Consultative Status with ECOSOC" Department of Economic and Social Affairs. http://www.un.org/esa/coordination/ngo/about.html (28 June, 2005)
(14) Hamad, et al. 2003.
(15) Gunter, Michael M. Jr. *Building the Next Ark: How NGOs work to Protect Biodiversity.* Dartmouth College Press, 2004.
(16) McKinley, E.H. *Marching to Glory: The History of The Salvation Army in the United States, 1880-1992.* William B. Eerdmans Publishing Company. Cambridge and Grand Rapids, 1995. Chapter 6.
(17) Hamad, et al, 2003.
(18) Hopgood, Stephen. *Keepers of the Flame: Understanding Amnesty International.* Cornell University Press, 2006.
(19) Hopgood, 2006.

Other Sources:

Bryant, Raymond L. *Nongovernmental Organizations in Environmental Struggles:*

The Way of the World

Politics and the Making of Moral Capital in the Philippines. Yale University Press, 2005.

Heere, Wybo P. Ed. *From Government to Governance: The Growing Impact of Non-state Actors on the International and European Legal System.* TMC Asser Press. The Hague, 2004.

Keck, Margaret E. and Kathryn Sikkink. *Activists Beyond Borders: Advocacy Networks in International Politics.* Cornell University Press. Ithaca, NY, 1998.

Martens, Kerstin. *NGOs and the United Nations: Institutionalization, Professionalization, and Adaptation.* Palgrave-McMillan. New York, 2005.

McCloskey, J. Michael. *In the Thick of It: My Life in the Sierra Club.* Island Press. Washington, 2005.

Minnear, Larry and Thomas G. Weiss. *Mercy Under Fire: War and the Global Humanitarian Community.* Westview. Boulder, CO, 1995.

Pease, Kelly-Kate S. *International Organizations: Perspectives on Governance in the Twenty-First Century.* Prentice Hall. New Jersey, 2000.

Raven, Peter H. "AIBS News: The Politics of Preserving biodiversity." *Bioscience* 40, No. 10. November 1990: 771.

Tickner, Joel, Carolyn Rafensperger, and Nancy Myers, "The Precautionary Principle in Action: A Handbook First Edition." Science and Environmental Health Network, May 31, 2003. http://www.biotech-info.net/precautionary.html.

Willets, Peter, Ed., *The Conscience of the World: The Influence of Non-Governmental Organizations in the UN System*. Hurst. London, 1996.

Benevolent Individuals Footnotes

(1) Gaudiani, Claire. *The Greater Good: How Philanthropy Drives the American Economy and Can Save Capitalism*. Times Books, 2003.
(2) Gaudiani, 2003: 2.
(3) Gaudiani, 2003.
(4) Fleishman, Joel L. "Philanthropic Leadership: A Personal Perspective." Presentation to HSBC Bank USA. http:/us.hsbc.com/privatebanking/wealth/pb_fleishman.asp.
(5) http://news.target.com/phoenix.zhtml?c=196187&p=irol-newsArticle&ID=932586
(6) Auletta, Ken. *Media Man: Ted Turner's Improbable Empire*. Atlas Books, 2004: 30.
(7) Auletta, 2004.
(8) Auletta, 2004.
(9) http://www.turnerfoundatin.org
(10) http://www.wikipedia.com (Jan 2007).
(11) http://www.oprah.com (Dec. 2006).
(12) http://www.learningtogive.org (Feb. 2007).
(13) Gaudiani, 2003: 17.

Other Sources:

Adam, Thomas, Ed. *Philanthropy, Patronage, and Civil Society: Experiences from Germany, Great Britain, and North America*. Indiana University Press, 2004.

Bonner, Michael, Mine Ener, Amy Singer, Eds. *Poverty and Charity in Middle Eastern Contexts*. State University of New York Press, 2003.

Clift, Elayne, Ed. *Women, Philanthropy, and Social Change: Vision for a just society*. Tufts University Press, 2005.

Creative Philanthropy: toward a new philanthropy for the 21st century.

De Borms, Luc Tayart. *Foundations: Creating Impact in a Globalised Worl.d* John Wiley & Sons, Ltd. 2005.

Gasman, Marybeth and Katherine V. Sedgwick Eds. *Uplifting a People*. Peter Lang. 2005.

Gregory, Robert G. *The Rise and Fall of Philanthropy in East Africa: The Asian Contribution*. Transaction Publishers, 1992.

Hopkins, Elwood M. *Collaborative Philanthropies: What Groups of Foundations Can Do that Individual Funders Cannot*. Lexington Books, Boulder. 2005.

Nagel, Stuart S Ed. *Eastern European Development and Public Policy*. St. Martin's Press. 1994.

Oliner, Samuel P. *Do Unto Others: Extraordinary Acts of Ordinary People*. Westview Press, 2003.

Organic Agriculture Footnotes

(1) Garcia, Deborah Koons. "The Future of Food." Motion Picture, 2001.
(2) Kuepper, George, and Lange Cegner. *Organic Crop Production Overview*. National Sustainable Agriculture Information Service. August 2004.
(3) Duram, Leslie A. *Good Growing: Why Organic Farming Works*. University of Nebraska Press, Lincoln and London, 2005.
(4) Berry, Wendell. *The Unsettling of America: Culture and Agriculture*. San Francisco. Sierra club Books, 1977. From Duram, Leslie A., 2005.
(5) Magdoff, F., JB Foster, and F. Buttel Eds. *Hungry for Profit: The Agribusiness Threat to Farmers, Food, and the Environment*. New York: Monthly Review Press, 2000.
(6) Jaffe, Gregory A. *Lessen the Fear of Genetically Engineered crops*. Christian Science Monitor, August 8, 2001:8.
(7) Magdoff, 2000.
(8) Pesticide Action Network of North America, 2003.
(9) Duram, 1994.
(10) Peter, D. and Ghesquiere, P. Bilan. *des connaissances et des applications de l'agriculture biologique et interet pour l'agriculture Communautaire*. Commission of the European Communities, Brussels, 1988.

(11) Lampkin, N.H. and S. Padel, Eds. *The Economics of Organic Farming: An International Perspective.* Cab International, Wallingford. 1994.
(12) Thompson, 2000.
(13) *Eco-Farming: The Chinese Experience.* Published through the United Nations Environment Program (UNEP).
(14) http://www.search.ers.USDA.gov (Jan 2007)
(15) Heaton, Shane. "Organic Farming, Food Quality, and Human Health Report. Briefing Sheet." UK Soil Association. 2001. http://www.soilassociation.org/web/sa/saweb.nsf/librarytitoles/Briefing_Sheets0308200a.
(16) Byrum, Allison. "Organically Grown Foods Higher in Cancer-Fighting Chemicals than Conventionally Grown Foods." American Chemical Society Public Release. March 3, 2003. http://www.eurekalert.org/pub_pubreleases/2003-03/acs-ogfo3o3o3.php.
(17) Grinder, 2003.
(18) Duram, 2003: 5
(19) Heaton, 2001
(20) Worthington, Virginia. "Effect of Agricultural Methods on Nutritional Quality: A comparison of Organic with Conventional Crops": *Alternative Therapies*, 1998. 4(1): 58-69. AND Worthington, Virginia. "Nutritional Quality of Organic Versus Conventional Fruits, Vegetables, and Grains." *Journal of Alternative and Complimentary Medicine.* 2001. 7(2): 161-173.
(21) Faeth, P., R. Repetto, K. Kroll, Q. Dai, and G. Helmers. *Paying the Farm Bill:U.S. Agricultural Policy and the Transition to Sustainable Agriculture.* World Resources Institute, Washington, D.C. 1991.

(22) OECD Working Papers. "Comparing the Profitability of Organic and Conventional Farming: The Impact of Support on Arable Farming in France," 2000.
(23) "Organic Agriculture and Rural Poverty Alleviation." Economic and Social Commission for Asia and the Pacific Potential and Best Practices in Asia. United Nations. New York, 2002.
(24) "Organic Agriculture and Rural Poverty Alleviation," 2002.

Other Sources:

Curl, Cynthia L. Richard A Fenske, and Kai Elgethun 2003. "Organi-phosphorous Pesticide Exposure of Urban and Suburban Preschool Children with organic and conventional diets." *Environmental Health Perspectives* 111(3): 377-382.

Dimitri, Carolyn, and Catherine Green. 2002. "Recent Growth Patterns in the US Organic Foods, Market." *USDA Economic Research Service, Agriculture Information Bulletin no. 777.*

Green, Catherine, and Amy Kremen. 2003. "US Organic Farming in 2000-2002: Adoption of Certified Systems." *USDA, Economic Research Service, Agriculture Information Bulletin no. 780.*

"Organic Food and Beverages: World Supply and Major European Markets." International Trade Centre, Geneva. 1999.

Pedersen, Lisbeth, S. Rasmussen, S. Bugel, L. Jargensen, L. Dragsted, V. Gundersen, and B Sandstrom. "Effects of Diets Based on Foods from Conventional Versus Organic Production and Intake and Excretion of Flavinoids and Markers of Defense in Humans." *Journal of Agricultural and Good Chemistry.* 2003. 51(19): 5671-76.

"World Markets for Organic Fruit and Vegetables: Opportunities for developing countries in the production and export of organic horticultural products." International Trade Centre, Technical Centre for Agricultural and Rural Cooperation. Food and Agriculture Organization of the United Nations Rome, 2001.

Worldwatch Paper 73. "Beyond the Green Revolution: New Approaches for Third World Agriculture." October, 1986.

http://www.wikipedia.org/wiki/organoponicos

Recycling Footnotes

(1) http://www.gothamgazette.com
(2) Curlee, T. Randal, Schexnayder, Vogt, Wolfe, Kelsay, and Feldman. *Waste to Energy in the United States: A social and economic assessment.* Quorum Books. 1994: 2.
(3) Kreith, Frank, Ed. *Handbook of Solid Waste Management.* McGraaw-Hill, 1994.
(4) Sayers, Dorothy L. "Why Work?" 1942.
(5) www.tufts.edu
(6) www.tufts.edu.
(7) California Integrated Waste Management Board (IWMB), California EPA.
(8) "City of Thousand Oaks: a model for local government recycling and waste reduction. 2002."
(9) IWMB, Thousand Oaks

(10) Kreith, 1994.
(11) California IWMB. "Resource Guide for Recycling-based Business. 1997": 37.
(12) *Biocycle Magazine* Annual Survey.
(13) California IWMB. "Organics Options: opportunities for local government reuse, recycling, and composting. 2002": 3.
(14) America's Second Harvest Website, 2002.
(15) California IWMB. "Last Chance Mercantile: A model for local government recycling and waste reduction. 2002": 1.
(16) Curlee, et al, 1994:12.
(17) California IWMB. "Commercial Innovations and Challenges: a model for local government recycling and waste reduction. 2002": 9.
(18) California IWMB. "Commercial Innovations and Challenges. 2002": 4.
(19) California IWMB. "Solid Waste Assessments: a model for local government recycling and waste reduction. 2002."
(20) California IWMB. "Taking Packaging for Granted: Can you afford to? 2007": 2.
(21) Ackerman, Frank. *Why Do We Recycle? Markets, Values, and Public Policy.* Island Press. 1997: 2.

Other Sources:

California Integrated Waste Management Board. "Feasibility Study on the Expanded Use of Agricultural and Forest Waste in Commercial Products. January 1999."

U.S. EPA. "The Solid Waste Dilemma: An Agenda for Action." Office of Solid Waste and Emergency Response. EPA/530-SW-89-019, February 1989.

Yen, T.F. Ed. *Recycling and Disposal of Solid Wastes: Industrial, agricultural, domestic.* Ann Arbor Science Publishers. 1974.

http://www.tufts.edu/tuftsrecycles/USstats.htm

Dependence on Oil Footnotes

(1) GJ Schwartz, Presentation to Southern California Vegan Society, July 2006.
(2) Pilger, John. *The New Rulers of the World.* Verso, London and New York, 2002.
(3) Pilger, 2002.
(4) Vidal, Gore. *Dreaming War: Blood for Oil and the Cheney/Bush Junta.* Nation Books. New York, 2003:13.
(5) Leech, Garry. *Crude Interventions: The United States, oil, and the new global (dis)order.* Zed Books. London and New York, 2006: 29.
(6) Leech, 2006: 32.
(7) Leech, 2006: 36.
(8) Gelbspan, Ross. *Boiling Point: How Politicians, Big Oil and Coal, Journalists, and Activists are Fueling the Climate Crisis – and What we can do to Avert Disaster.* Basic Books. New York, 2004.
(9) Gelbspan, 2004.
(10) Bykoff, Maxwell T. and Jules M. "Balance as Bias: Global Warming and the U.S. Prestige Press." *Global Environmental Change* (14) 2004. 125-136.
(11) Harper's Index 2003.
(12) Gelbspan, 2004: 51.

(13) Klare, Michael T. *Blood and Oil: the dangers and consequences of America's Growing Dependency.* Henry Hold and Company, 2004: 59.
(14) Gelbspan, 2004: 70, 72.
(15) Gelbspan, 2004: 69.
(16) http://www.greenpeace.org

Other Sources:

Everest, Larry. *Oil Power, and Empire: Iraq and the US Global Agenda.* Common Courage Press 2004.

Klare, Michael T. *Resource Wars: the New Landscape of Global Conflict.* Henry Holt and Company. New York, 2001.

Miller, David Ed. *Tell Me Lies: propaganda and media distortion in the attack on Iraq.* Pluto Press, 2004.

Miniter, Richard. *Shadow War: the Untold Story of How Bush is Winning the War on Terror.* Regnery Publishing, Inc. Washington, D.C. 2004.

Pelletiere, Stephen. *America's Oil Wars.* Praeger, 2004.

Scott, Peter Dale. *Drugs, Oil, and War.* Rowan & Littlefield, 2003.

Sperry, Paul. *Crude Politics.* WND Books, 2003.

Yetiv, Steve A. *Crude Awakenings: Global Oil Security and American Foreign Policy.* Cornell University Press, 2004.

The So-Called Drug War Footnotes

(1) Bulmer-Thomas, Victor, and James Dunkerley, Eds. *The United States and Latin America: The New Agenda.* Institute of Latin American Studies at University of London, 1999.
(2) Gerber, Jurg, and Eric L. Jensen, Ed. *Drug War American Style.* Garland. New York, 2001.
(3) Bulmer-Thomas, 1999: 162.
(4) Amnesty International 1990: 70.
(5) Huggins, M.K. "Vigilantism and the State in Modern Latin America," in M.K. Huggins Ed., *U.S. Supported State Terror – A History of Police Training in Latin America* (pp. 219-242) Praeger. New York, 1991.
(6) Gerber, 2001: 182
(7) www.whitehousedrugpolicy.gov
(8) www.colombiasupport.net

Other Sources:

Allen, Christian M. *An Industrial Geography of Cocaine.* Routledge, 2005.

Bagley, Bruce M., and William O. Walker III, Eds. *Drug trafficking in the Americas. Transaction Publishers, 1994.*

Joyce, Elizabeth and Carlos Melanuel, Eds. *Latin America and the Multi-national Drug Trade.* MacMillan Press, 1988.

Mabry, Donald J. Ed. *The Latin American Narcotics Trade and US National Security.* Greenwood Press. Westport, CT, 1989.

MacDonald, Scott B. *Dancing on a Volcano*. Praeger, 1988.

Morales, Edmundo. *Cocaine: White Gold Rush in Peru*. University of Arizona Press, 1989.

Murillo, Mario A. *Colombia and the United States: War, Unrest, and Destabilization*. Seven Stories Press. New York, 2004.

Vellinga, Menno, Ed. *The Political Economy of the Drug Industry: Latin America and the International System*. University Press of Florida, Gainsville, 2004.

Zirnite, P. "The Militarization of the Drug War in Latin America." *Current History* 97: 166-173. 1998.

Human Traffic Footnotes

(1) UN estimates, found in State Department Trafficking in Persons Report, 2003.
(2) Clawson, David L. and Merrill L. Johnson. *World Regional Geography: A development approach*. Prentice Hall, 2003: 510.
(3) "Owed Justice: Thai Women Trafficked into Debt Bondage in Japan." Human Rights Watch. New York. Washington, 2000.
(4) "Owed Justice," 2000: 6.
(5) Skrobanek, Siriphon, Nattaya Bookpakdi, and Chutima Janthakeero. *The traffic in women: human realities of the international sex trade*. Zed Books. London, 1997.

(6) Asia Migrant Bulletin. July-December, 1995. Volume III. No. 3&4.
(7) Williams, Phil, Ed. *Illegal Immigration and Commercial Sex: The New Slave Trade.* Frank Cass. London, 1999.
(8) Williams, 1999.
(9) Clawson and Johnson, 2003.
(10) UN estimates, 2003.
(11) "Owed Justice," 2000: 25-26.
(12) UN estimates, 2003.
(13) Bush plan chronology taken from: Troubnikoff, Anna M. Ed. *Trafficking in Women and Children: Current Issues and Developments*, Nova Publishing, New York, 2003.
(14) Clinton plan chronology taken from Troubnikoff, 2003.
(15) http://www.usinfo.state.gov/gi/Archive/2004/May/1 2-381449.html
(16) Campagna, Daniel S., and Donald L. Poffenberger. *The Sexual Trafficking in Children: An Investigation of the Child Sex Trade.* Auburn House, Dover, Mass. 1988.

Other Sources:

Jeffrey, Leslie Ann. *Sex and Borders: Gender, National Identity, and Prostitution Policy in Thailand.* UBC Press. Vancuver, 2002.

Kempadoo, Kamala, and Doezema Jo. *Global Sex Workers: Rights, Resistance, and Redefinition.* Routledge, New York, 1998.

Pattanaik, Bandana, and Susanne Thorbek, Eds. *Transnational Prostitution: changing global patterns*. Zed Books. London, 2002: 123.

Seabrook, Jeremy. *Travels in the Skin Trade: Tourism and the Sex Industry*. Pluto Press. London, 2001.

Steady, Filomina Chioma. *Black Women, Globalization, and Economic Justice: Studies from Africa and the African Diaspora*. Schenkman Books. Rochester, Vermont, 2002.

Printed in the United States
135055LV00002B/2/A